Feeling and
Imagination

Books by Irving Singer

Feeling and Imagination: The Vibrant Flux
of Our Existence

Sex: A Philosophical Primer

Explorations in Love and Sex (Forthcoming)

George Santayana, Literary Philosopher

Reality Transformed: Film as Meaning and Technique

Meaning in Life:
The Creation of Value
The Pursuit of Love
The Harmony of Nature and Spirit

The Nature of Love:
Plato to Luther
Courtly and Romantic
The Modern World

Mozart and Beethoven: The Concept of Love
in Their Operas

The Goals of Human Sexuality

Santayana's Aesthetics

Essays in Literary Criticism by George Santayana (editor)

The Nature and Pursuit of Love: The Philosophy of
Irving Singer (edited by David Goicoechea)

Feeling and Imagination

The Vibrant Flux of Our Existence

Irving Singer

ROWMAN & LITTLEFIELD PUBLISHERS, INC.
Lanham • Boulder • New York • London

ROWMAN & LITTLEFIELD PUBLISHERS, INC.

Published in the United States of America
by Rowman & Littlefield Publishers, Inc.
4720 Boston Way, Lanham, Maryland 20706
www.rowmanlittlefield.com

12 Hid's Copse Road
Cumnor Hill, Oxford OX2 9JJ, England

British Cataloging in Publication Information Available

Library of Congress Cataloging-in-Publication Data

Singer, Irving.
    Feeling and imagination : the vibrant flux of our existence / Irving Singer.
        p. cm.
    Includes bibliographical references and index.
    ISBN 0-7425-1234-7 (cloth : alk. paper)
        1. Emotions. 2. Emotions and cognition. 3. Affect (Psychology) I. Title.

BF531 .S58 2001
128'.3—dc21

                                                                    00-065325

Printed in the United States of America

∞^{TM} The paper used in this publication meets the minimum
requirements of American National Standard for Information
Sciences—Permanence of Paper for Printed Library Materials,
ANSI/NISO Z39.48-1992.

To Dick,
Who always kept the faith,
And to the memory of
Beloved Catherine

Contents

Preface

The world is not a tragedy or a comedy: it is a flux.
—George Santayana, letter to Charles P. Davis, April 3,
1936.

I have had a most rare vision. . . . The eye of man hath not
heard, the ear of man hath not seen, man's hand is not able
to taste, his tongue to conceive, nor his heart to report,
what my dream was. I will get Peter Quince to write a
ballad of this dream: it shall be called Bottom's Dream,
because it hath no bottom.
—William Shakespeare, *A Midsummer Night's Dream*, Act
IV, Scene 1.

In this book I try to show how we create our world, in part,
through what we call our "feelings." That catchall word
covers a large variety of attitudes, dispositions, sentiments,
emotions, intuitions, inclinations, and kinesthetic sensations.
The inevitable vagueness or ambiguity to which it leads may
explain why the subject is often ignored by professional
philosophers. With their legitimate concern for precision

and rigorous analysis, they have gravitated toward issues that seem to promise a more reliable resolution.

In our age of esteem for the accomplishments of science and technology, we tend to neglect humanistic fields that are inherently different, even though the humanities often emulate cognitive procedures that are essential in these other disciplines. Writing as a humanistic philosopher, I offer a view of the affective dimension in our being which supplements, but does not duplicate, scientific inquiry. Feeling always exists in some interaction with cognitive structures. It cannot be wholly separated from them. Yet it typically lends itself to an approach that is more characteristic of the humanities than of the sciences. That is the approach I take.

I have previously made forays into the realm of affect in my writings on love, sex, compassion, and conditions such as friendship and a religious or cosmic sense of oneness. In this book I want to cut across the gamut of human feeling, inspecting it more fully though sometimes with concepts that I broached in those earlier stages of development. By portraying how feeling relies upon imagination, and through imagination upon idealization, consummation, and the aesthetic, I attempt to draw a family picture that will present the basic lineaments of sex, love, and compassion as well as the other stations of the spectrum to which they belong.

The introductory chapter places the succeeding ones in a context of ideas about feeling in general and, more specifically, attachment of the sort that some psychologists have been investigating for the last forty years. The final chapter considers how affective failures and imperfect attachments can play a constructive role in the growth of imagination, idealization, consummation, and the aesthetic— each of which reveals the vibrancy of our existence. In their complexity they give meaning to life and make it worth living.

Throughout the book I employ the term *affective attachment* in a way that requires prior explanation. One might say that all attachment—all bonding between human beings, for instance—is inherently affective. To this extent, the concept of affective attachment would seem to be redundant. Nevertheless we also know that, in itself and in its causal or other consequences, attachment always has cognitive implications. Though these are worth studying and are clearly important for understanding human nature and conduct, they are not the focus of my attention. Nor is the fact that some affective responses have little or no relevance to any search for attachment. A feeling of queasiness after a heavy meal does not indicate a failed attachment. But a sense of malaise in returning to one's childhood home may very well signify that a former attachment there was not entirely satisfying. The parameters of my subject in these pages are defined by the overlap between affect and attachment, the part of affective life which is pertinent to the phenomenon of attachment and the part of that phenomenon which directly involves our feelings in themselves and in their relation to whatever cognitive elements that may also exist.

The chapters that follow should be read as a single unfolding of speculative thought. Each of them is incomplete without the others. In one place Rousseau begs the indulgence of his readers by noting—as if it were a problem only he had to face—that he cannot say everything at once. My situation is comparable but more extreme. I find that our affective being is so mercurial that touching on it at a single point quickly precipitates volatile excursions that often rebound in unforeseeable directions. This is reflected in the exploratory nature of my writing. It is moreover how the world appears to me, and how its creative and bottomless flux may also exist even in those who choose not to concern themselves with this aspect of our being. I hope to induce in my readers something like the sense of astonishment that has motivated the composition of this text.

Among the people who helped me with the book, in one way or another, I am especially grateful to James D. Cain, Herbert Engelhardt, James Engell, Cándido Pérez Gállego, Felipe Guardiola, Malte Herwig, Leonard D. Katz, Alan P. Lightman, Richard A. Macksey, Timothy J. Madigan, Arnold H. Modell, Lianne Newton, Josephine F. Singer, Robert C. Solomon, Michael Wager, and Matthew G. Yurkewych.

I. S.

Introduction

Affective Attachments

In recent years academic psychologists have started to direct their experimental and observational expertise toward the scientific study of feeling. Fruitful as their work may be in relation to the cognitive methods they employ, it tends to ignore the nature of human attachments and the role that affect plays in them. In my estimation, that is an unfortunate development. Several decades ago, proponents of the "object-relations" school of psychiatry examined affective attachment from a somewhat different point of view. I will presently review their ideas, but as a prelude to my approach throughout this book I begin with a representative example of attachments that pervade an aesthetic activity many people care about.[1]

Think of a singer who performs in a concert of rock music, in a church, in an opera, or in a recital of art songs, whether she is a soloist or a member of the chorus. The singer tries to initiate and experience different kinds of felt rapport—with her listeners in the audience, obviously, but also with the conductor, if there is one, with her accompanists in the orchestra or at the piano, with fellow artists in a vocal ensemble, and above all with the music itself. In these different types of implied or explicit attachment every accomplished singer must possess a variety of cognitive talents requisite for this art form. Great singers are those who can employ such talents to near perfection. But they must also be proficient in articulating and evoking feelings that are crucial for their individual presentation.

The intellect of singers, as of dancers, is often denigrated by people who have verbal and critical skills superior to theirs. Yet performers could not excel in their chosen medium unless they had intellectual powers of considerable proportion. For one thing, they need to be sophisticated about the techniques that define their art form. They must also know how to communicate ideas as well as feelings to persons unlike themselves. They must know how to *perform*, how to appear before others in a manner that binds them to their audience in each production. They must learn to use their bodies effectively, to breathe or look or walk or run in the artificial but meaningful manner demanded by their self-expression in whatever role or artistic posture they assume.

These, and other aptitudes one can easily imagine, do not occur in isolation. They are components, cognitive and affective, within offerings that express and convey a performer's sense of reality. The cognitive has little aesthetic importance except in relation to the feelings that a work of art embodies and refines in its own fashion. The singer is engaged in an enterprise that directs her cognitive capacity toward affective goals attainable through the vocal medium. Her performance is sustained by consummations she experiences immediately and in the company of those for whom she sings. Her activity is a type of attachment behavior that can be life-enhancing for herself as well as for her listeners.

But to what, exactly, is she attached? That question, philosophical and somewhat elusive, is reminiscent of the famous one that William Butler Yeats asks at the end of his poem "Among School Children." I alter it to read: "How can we know the singer from the song?"[2] When musical attachment succeeds, the performer and the sounds he or she makes are joined in an affective unity that is sought in all aesthetic experience, though significantly different in each art form. A sense of the oneness that may occur on some occasion is experienced by both the artist and the audience.

Even so, the feelings involved, evident and authentic as they may be, require much analysis before they can reveal the nature of their affective import. In attempting this analysis, we can possibly take our reference point in an individual's distant past. As specialists in child development, psychologists may validly focus upon that stage of life even though adults generally forget most of what happened then. Since everyone starts his or her existence as a dependent infant seeking the physical and psychological protection that only a mature person can provide, some investigators maintain that childhood attachments carry over into interests that determine our affective being in each later period. If this is true, the attachments ingredient in the singer's art must originate in the buried residue of infancy and then continue throughout the intervening years. Most theorists nowadays are careful to avoid *reducing* adult attitudes to something that happened in childhood. But many of them believe that essentially, inherently, the present shows forth the past as a result of attachment patterns that are formed soon after birth.

While this assumption can serve as a basis for the empirical work these scientists do, there is another point of view that one can have. By examining an adult's affective response at any present moment, we can more reliably discern the operative dynamism in that person's experience as it currently exists. It often differs greatly from anything that might be adduced by studying affective dispositions in the past.

Following this methodology, I call attention to the singer's feelings while she sings—her feelings about herself, but also her feelings about the auditory, kinesthetic, visual, and other sensations that comprise her intuition of what is happening in her mind and body as she sings. Her ability to accept herself as the social and sexual being that she is will affect the quality of her singing, especially in public where she and her performance are exposed to the glare of enjoyment-seeking strangers. In addition to training pupils in solfeggio and how to breathe or control the larynx, at least one singing teacher that I have known encourages them to project their voice as if it came from their genitals as well as from their diaphragm and mouth.

The accomplished attachment of a singer to her art, and her possible oneness with the song she sings, is a consummation of her musical talent. As in any other artistic venture, singing is a contrivance for transforming nature through aesthetic possibilities. These appear in the expressiveness of feelings or emotions as they communicate values that matter to human beings and therefore constitute the human spirit. The singer who is secure within her physical and psychological state creates this attachment as a means of reaching people for whom, and with whom, she is singing. Her successful presentation of the music will come into being only if her personhood infuses the sounds she produces with an affective resonance her listeners can detect and enjoy responsively whether or not they have had the same experience themselves.

The consummations that may ensue, each in its own domain, help us understand why so many people love, and give themselves to, the difficult art of singing. Whatever their causal origin, the aesthetic attachments can certainly resemble childhood feelings toward a mother or father. Teachers, coaches, and conductors often fill that quasi-parental role for singers and other performing artists. But they do so under conditions that lie beyond any childhood need. At their best, they induce consummatory bonds of another sort.

I have chosen the vocal art to illustrate this characteristic syndrome because singing is exceptional in depending upon bodily and mental proclivities that virtually everyone has. We all talk and use our voice expressively; we all exchange feelings and ideas through language that is phonetically inflected (hence musical to that degree); we all present ourselves to others through the meaningful utterances that issue from our lips; we all display in these daily performances the ideals and personal aspirations that manifest our conception of what life is and ought to be. In the art of singing, people cultivate and complete these potentialities of our species through sonic inventions that some composer or folk tradition has made available.

Though they usually need years of training and assistance from others in order to master the great expressiveness of music, singers are nevertheless their own instruments. In effecting a panoramic attachment to those who treasure their artistry, they become attached not only to the sensations, the emotions, the feelings, and the thoughts of these people but also to themselves as vehicles of interpersonal contact merely in being what they are and doing what only they can do. This is a fountainhead of creative power as well as security and ability to survive.

At the same time, we must remember that something comparable can exist with the aid of instruments that are not ourselves but manufactured. The person who clutches a clarinet, or pounds a drum, or modulates across a keyboard, or nestles a harp or cello between his legs can experience a range of attachments not wholly different from the singer's. Though indirectly, these nonvocal performers are also their own instruments. In becoming appendages to the ones they play upon, they are simultaneously making these objects appendages to the cognitive and affective forces within themselves as musicians. In sister arts like dance and theater, performers are their own instruments as in singing, but through talents that subordinate the sonic dimension to other creative possibilities.

I am suggesting that affective attachments should be studied as meaningful forms of life that cannot be explained entirely by reference to what happens in childhood. Singing is not the same as playing the piano, but each enables us to effect types of consummatory oneness that exceed those that a child might hope to get from its caretaker. Musical instruments are artifacts of technology, akin to a camera that a teenager wears about the neck like an amulet of attachment, or the laptop computer to which I, at least, am intimately bonded. I feel gratitude, even love, for its serviceability in eliciting ideas that arise when I type on it. The child's enjoyment of the comfort and support offered by its mother's bountiful body may be analogous. But much else must also be considered before we can understand the universal tendency to become attached to arts and technologies. In their total impact they transcend the affective realities of our early years.

If we think of human life as basically aesthetic and even able to become a work of art, we begin to see why a new approach to affect and attachment can be useful. Like the singer, athletes and men or women of action are their own instruments, though they too depend on technologies they employ. Almost all of our existence may be similar in that respect. With this as our guiding principle, we can then search for conceptions that may possibly elucidate it.

❋

In this pursuit, we should consider a major turning point in the history of psychiatric theory that occurred shortly after the end of World War II. Freud had finished his work almost ten years before. Even his most devoted followers were questioning many of his ideas. Those who believed in the object-relations view of human nature promised a new beginning for psychoanalysis.

Melanie Klein, D. W. Winnicott, and W. R. D. Fairbairn belonged to this group. Instead of treating drives or instincts as fundamental constants, they considered them variable devices for establishing viable relationships with meaningful and valued objects. Denying any primacy of sexual impulse, for instance, the new point of view emphasized the child's search for security attainable through bonding with a caretaker who could help him or her to survive and to flourish in the world.

This major difference between the old-line Freudian position and the burgeoning orientation that wished to revise it may serve as an introduction to subsequent theories about the nature of attachment. These theories arose as an application of the object-relations approach. They were largely developed by John Bowlby and followers of his such as Mary D. S. Ainsworth, Peter Marris, and Robert S. Weiss.[3] Among Bowlby's many adherents they are particularly noteworthy since they extended his thinking into areas he had left unexplored. Bowlby studied the ways in which small children bond with a mother who can afford safety and protection, but Ainsworth put youngsters into situations that were strange to them. Marris examined the cultural implications of human attachments. Weiss applied the concept of attachment to adult as well as childhood relationships.

Bowlby and the others believed that attachment is a behavioral system composed of cognitive as well as affective elements relevant to it. As cognitive, attachment yields information and awareness that helps an organism to cope with the vicissitudes in life. As affective, attachment includes a range of feelings that indicate the level of progress in this endeavor. In the words of one commentator: "To feel attached is to feel safe and secure. By contrast, . . . insecurely attached persons may have a mixture of feelings towards their attachment figure: intense love and dependency, fear of rejection, irritability and vigilance. One may theorize that their lack of security has aroused a simultaneous wish to be close and the angry determination to punish their attachment figure for the minutest sign of abandonment."[4]

In the present and later chapters I adapt this conception of attachment to fit my philosophical exploration. Extending the work of Bowlby and his successors for that purpose, I add little to the scientific data that they or other attachment theorists have amassed. Nor can I pretend that my reflections strengthen their observational insights. Instead I hope to supplement their research, as well as the current work in the cognitive psychology of affect, by enclosing it within a more comprehensive view. I argue that in human experience cognition is always correlative to some affective need, and to relevant attachments of one type or another. Though my approach is humanistic, phenomenological, and not scientific, it is fully amenable to all that has been achieved by different social scientists in these fields of inquiry.

I emphasize the nonscientific quality of my perspective because much of what I say does not lend itself to precise quantification or controlled replication. Affective attachment, as I envisage it, is a baffling and even mysterious fact of our nature. That two persons, or a person and an object, or a person and an ideal, can be bound together by the affective ties that are common in our species should make us wonder about our reality. Elsewhere I liken this erotic glue to the force of gravity in the physical world. We know very little about either. Trying to make sense of "the erotic," I contrasted it with "the libidinal" and "the romantic."[5] These interwoven attitudes constitute what we experience as human sexuality or love. They are greatly dissimilar among themselves. Regardless of how we define the libidinal, no one would claim that the bonding between an infant and its caretaker contains the same carnal interest as exists between two adults who crave genital intercourse with each other. Nor can attachments established in the first years of life be reduced to romantic inclinations. These involve ideas about the individuality of the other person as well as a desire for permanent and pervasive closeness. But such ideas can occur only after much acculturation in a society that is conceptually and historically receptive to it.

While the erotic often operates in harmony with the libidinal and the romantic, it is not reducible to either of them. The erotic has a special kind of tug. Causing us to gravitate within the orbit of some person, thing, or ideal that attracts us, it often appears as curiosity or gregariousness, and sometimes as moral concern focused upon this other entity. The erotic is inherently an aesthetic response. Not only is it alert to physical or spiritual beauties but also it comprises an unbridled flow of imagination that human beings have more extensively than other organisms, and frequently apart from libidinal or romantic feelings. In a preliminary fashion, attachment may be envisaged as a subdivision of the erotic.

For some philosophers, even this tentative statement will seem problematic. The erotic pertains to sex or sexual love, they may remark, but are we prepared to think that attachment between an infant and its caretaker must be described in that way? To accommodate the fact that overt libidinal drive cannot account for all the relationships that bind people to each other, Freud developed the notions of sublimation and aim-inhibited sex. In avoiding his tactic, my view would seem to be more radically pansexual. If attachment is linked to the erotic, which is an element of sex, am I not portraying all affective bonds as sexual to that extent?

I am not distressed by this interpretation, provided it is correctly formulated. To recognize a sexual aspect in some experience that may seem to be purely mental or even spiritual is indeed to see our nature in a manner that contravenes traditional doctrines. But the troublesome view is worthy of consideration. A pansexual perspective is faulty only if we identify sexuality with the libidinal. Once our pluralistic stance takes us beyond that reduction, however, we become sensitive to humanity's immersion in the realm of matter even when it is able to rise above materiality alone.[6]

The erotic is embedded in the material, as all of sex is, but it also awakens nonphysical reactions. It does this by creating feelings and cognitive constructions that incline us toward the varied attributes of persons, things, and ideals, attributes that are often so vague and remote in our awareness as to seem as if they emanate from a spiritual domain "outside of nature." Our language is insufficiently refined to shield us from such modes of talking and, therefore, thinking. But to that degree ordinary discourse is misleading. Spirit is a part of nature. It is nature at its highest, its most valuable configuration gauged by standards native to ourselves. Sexuality readily lends itself to both the natural and the spiritual. It is the energy, the vibrant impulse, the longing and emotional power that joins the two. Sex is what Verdi called "la forza del destino," the *force*—as in the *Star Wars* cycle—that propels whatever destiny human beings engender or accept and thus create as the value of their lives.

With this as our conception of sexuality, we need only determine how its components operate and interact. There is no single, uniform pattern that this interaction takes. It alters with changing interests and varying attachments. Since we have ruled out the notion that our behavior can be explained solely in terms of the libidinal, we do well to ask when and how much that type of sex enters into human existence. Sometimes very little, sometimes quite a lot, whether or not we recognize its hidden influence. Each case must be analyzed on its own, which need not keep us from believing that sexuality of *some* kind—occasionally the romantic, but usually the erotic in one form or another—is present on all occasions.

I think Plato would have accepted this conception of sexuality and the erotic. It encompasses much of what he meant by *Eros*. At times Freud seemed to be moving toward conclusions not unlike the ones I am sketching here. Toward the end of his career Freud expressed amazement at the suggestion that he reduced all motivation to the demands of an ultimate and pervasive sex drive. He remarked that the word he used for sexuality was *Liebe*, which in German also means "love." But Freud was disingenuous in saying this, since his theory tendentiously interprets love as sex and sex as libido, albeit often aim-inhibited.

Nevertheless I take Freud's latter-day disclaimer as revealing that he saw a weakness in his official teaching.

Though he did not rectify the deficiency, he must have surmised that if Liebe signifies love this is worth stating only because love involves something different from libido, whether or not its aim is inhibited. An acceptable theory of either love or sex would have to reveal the basic plurality in both and why it is that each exceeds, in fact transcends, any libidinal elements it may also include. Freud does not give us this type of theory. Far from tending toward it, the concept of sublimation that he offers serves only to mask its absence from his general outlook.

The philosophical project I wish to undertake has been hampered by methodological attitudes that were, and still are, prevalent in this field. I already mentioned the mistake of thinking that all attachments arise from those that exist in infancy or childhood. Even if we spurn, as Bowlby does, the attempt to reduce adult attachments to events that exist in early years, it is erroneous to overemphasize the importance of what may have happened in the past but is now unfathomable. We know, of course, that much of life is molded by habit formation, and we know that habits are strongest when they date back to the time when some affective response first comes into being. But we also know that these responses are always subject to such extensive transformations that totally new coordinates must be invoked to understand attachments, or searchings for attachment, that may occur later on.

The failure to heed this scruple is sometimes called "the genetic fallacy." It is often accompanied by another that persists even among scientists who try to avoid being reductivistic in their theory construction. While agreeing that no one mode of analysis can explain everything, some scientists assume that all phenomena are knowable in principle—if only they are studied long enough and with the most advanced techniques that science can attain. This view is a kind of cosmic reductivism that ignores the latent and changing creativity that pervades the world as a whole. The effects of thinking that science probes into a fixed and rigid universe whose ultimate workings may someday be disclosed are especially disconcerting in relation to questions about attachment. For that is always in flux, and largely unpredictable. At the end of this book, I return to the perils of believing that reality—above all, the reality of our affective experience—is fundamentally the same and capable of being fully known by us.

Finally, we should note a common confusion about the role of speculative models in studying the nature of human attachment. They are often treated as a by-product of our species' vast capacity to formulate theories of any kind, whether practical or abstract, that presuppose the primacy of cognition. Particularly in the Anglo-Saxon countries but also in other regions of the globe, as I remarked earlier, the current orthodoxy in science and philosophy has generally avoided humanistic approaches to the nature of affect. They are thought to be either unmanageable or else themselves subject to the same cognitive methodology that has given us knowledge about impersonal matters of fact. And, unquestionably, much has been achieved in the growth and refinement of the dominant outlook. But the random attempts to apply it to the study of feeling, or of value, leave a great deal that still needs to be done. That is the challenge for humanist as well as nonhumanist philosophers, now and in the future.

Some time ago I took a step in this direction by offering a distinction between "appraisal" and "bestowal." I described them as different modes of valuation that normally appear together in everyday life. I used these concepts to explain the nature of love as the valuing of some person, thing, or ideal. Though I did not fully develop this idea, I believed that sexuality and related matters would also lend themselves to my type of analysis. I have since concluded that any bonding can be seen as involving both appraisal and bestowal. While love and sex exemplify human attachment, whether complete or incomplete, consummatory or frustrated as it may be, most other affective patterns can also be treated as conglomerates of appraisal and bestowal.

By appraisal I mean the act of discovering what something is worth to us or others in view of self-oriented interests that we or they may have. Appraisal is thus a form of inductive reasoning about the availability of satisfaction. It judges the goodness or badness of someone or some thing, and determines its value, by reference to the ability of that person or object to provide whatever people want. Appraisal may be instantaneous or prolonged, conscious or unconscious, directed toward a single attribute or toward a total entity. If the putative worth is or can be assessed in terms of benefits to a community of human beings, I call the valuation "objective appraisal." If the value is idiosyncratic to oneself, established in accordance with one's own needs and desires even if no one else has them, I refer to the valuation as an "individual appraisal."

Bestowal is a different type of valuing. Instead of asking how someone can be of use to us or others, bestowal creates value by accepting that person as is, whatever he or she happens to be and apart from considerations of self-interest that we ourselves may have. Through bestowal the recipient of our attention is valued over and above its appraised goodness. It is treated *as if* some appraisal found it to be excellent, even perfect, though no such appraisal has been made or can occur. This act of imagination, this imaginative way of responding affirmatively to a person, or a thing, or an ideal, constitutes our capacity for bestowal and makes its beneficiary valuable in that respect. At length and in many contexts, I tried to see and to show how love involves the constant interaction between bestowal and individual or objective appraisal. I sought to delineate the conditions under which the two modalities combine in a joint, though often dissonant, unification that we recognize as the experience of love.[7]

By applying similar analyses to attachment, we may acquire conceptual tools that clarify the role of affect in human life as a whole. Feelings are not just reactions to external objects that interest us because of their utility or threat to our survival. Affectivity is also a *making* of importance, a bestowing of value by virtue of our attachment itself. No one can be attached through appraisiveness alone, however attractive the beguiling object may be. For a relationship to matter, a person, thing, or ideal must be treated as inherently meaningful, and not just instrumentally valuable. The man or woman must be accepted as he or she is, in his or her indefeasible reality, which includes appraised value but is not limited to that. By its very nature, attachment consists of nascent or developed bestowals as well as appraisals. Therein lies both its affective and its cognitive significance.

Bowlby and others in his school perceive that attachment is not a mechanistic device, as Freud seemed to think, but rather part of a quest for meaning in one's life. Nevertheless, Bowlby and the others often describe attachment in the language of appraisal. They interpret the child's longing for a mother or surrogate caretaker in terms of its need to survive and feel secure. As one discussant says: "In Bowlby's original formulation, natural danger cues (e.g., noise, strangeness, rapid approach, isolation) activate

attachment behavior through the arousal of fear. . . .
Ainsworth emphasized that the child's appraisal of the
relative presence of threat and security plays a significant
role in the behavioral balance of exploration, affiliation,
wariness, and attachment that the child demonstrates."[8]

The existence of the appraisive coordinates cited by
Bowlby and Ainsworth need not be doubted. But it would be
a mistake to ignore the extent to which attachment involves
much more as well. The bond these investigators have
studied so carefully consists of bestowals that enable
attachment to function as it does in human existence.
Bestowal makes attachments meaningful through its own
creative agency as an expression of personal and social
feeling. It evinces imaginative projections that must be
examined in their great variety. I try to do so throughout the
subsequent chapters. While seeking this explication, we can
retain most of the behavioral and ethological data that
Bowlby, Ainsworth, and their fellow scientists proffer. We
need only supplement their work with conceptual
refinements that add another dimension to their observations.

Studying affect and attachment, one has a tendency to
concentrate upon the positive aspects of each. Philosophers
often sound that way in their writing. We conceive of human
nature in relation to the ideals that people variably
construct in all societies; and though we know how hard it
is for men and women to satisfy these aspirations through
which they create themselves, we do not always depict their
frequent failures as thoroughly as we should. This
shortcoming may possibly result from our professional
preoccupation with ideas and their ingredient contents.
Having analyzed a concept, we tend to ask: Must I now

enumerate everything that *defeats* its definition? Not at all, and yet negativities can also elucidate the positive. Though we define love or compassion as a form of benevolence and benign acceptance, we enrich our comprehension of these noble states when we see them as concomitant to anger, hatred, and aggression. These are always relevant.

Realist thinkers like Freud and many social scientists argue that all affective attachments are predicated upon negative as well as affirmative responses. The detailed merits of that thesis must be argued independently. As a possible generalization, however, it is a working hypothesis we may keep in mind. What remains to be discovered is *how* the positive and the negative are bound to each other, how they interact with each other, assuming that they do, and how they may be unified, harmonized, in the struggle for supervening goals that human beings treasure.

Our theme must therefore emphasize affective failure as well as success. In chapters 1 through 4 of this book, I discuss elements of our being—imagination, idealization, consummation, the aesthetic—that pertain to affect at its most affirmative. They are prominent in attainments that can make life worth living and promise a happy as well as a meaningful existence. They are experienced as glowing realities that give hope and enable us to go on as we wish. But behind them, and within them as well, there resides the darkened lining of negative feelings destructive to human welfare. We all shun the necessity of facing up to this. The greatest tragedy in life results from wanting to have the maximum of happiness and meaning without being reconciled to the unremitting strife, discomfort, and abhorrent labor that is usually inseparable from it.

In one place Nietzsche remarks: "Deeply do I love life— and verily, most of all when I hate life."[9] Did he mean that his love of life overcomes and somehow eradicates his

hatred of it, or was he saying that such love cannot be
distinguished from, is ineluctably fused with, some
correlative hatred toward the life he also loves? I return to
this problem in the last chapter. Here it can suggest some of
the background that I presuppose on every page of this
book.

Several other questions about the multifarious quality of
affective attachment are also worth mentioning in advance.
If there is an inner dialectic between its positive and
negative components, how can failure lead to success, defeat
to renewal, hatred to love, anger or bitterness to the
consummation of tender feelings and mutual concern? Is it
possible that anger, for instance, is itself consummatory and
an attunement to something deeply imbedded in our
reality? Given what we are as human beings, can anger
somehow attach us to a world that cares little about our
existence and will someday annihilate it? When our cosmic
fury is turned upon some hapless fellow victim in the misery
of life, does it express legitimate resentment toward our fate
in being finite and relatively fragile? Is it a way of stating:
"This is how things are, the horrible truth is there before
you, it is no longer hidden, my hostile sentiments reveal
what I am like, take them as you wish"?

Persons who feel and behave like that are generally
considered too difficult to live with. But sometimes their
proud, though virulent, defiance has been admired as an
authentic recognition of what we are by nature. These
individuals may even become objects of attachment and
affective fascination that some people interpret as a form of
love. I am thinking of Byronic heroes in fiction, for example,
Heathcliff in *Wuthering Heights* or recent cinematic
personifications of mad though metaphysical rage, such as
Dr. Lecter in *The Silence of the Lambs*. Some women fall
passionately in love with one after another of these

tormented but sadistic weaklings. In analyzing the negativity that accompanies whatever is positive in affective attachments, we must ask ourselves whether and why each mode of failure does or does not generate some corresponding success.

Moreover, failure in some affective system (sex, let us say) may often lead to successful attachments in other areas of life—in friendship love, artistic creativity, social fulfillment either as a consummate sybarite or as the savior of one's people. What is there within feeling or attachment that underlies these transformational potentialities?

While keeping such questions before us, we should not assume that all attachments can be transformed. Failure in one modality may not always be remediable by success of an alternate kind. As there is no single, unitary pattern that defines the nature of love, or sex, or compassion, or any other affective response, neither is there a uniform essence in attachment as a whole. For that reason, we should not expect to find an a priori assurance that every failure can be outweighed by an ultimate and happy resolution provided by some other person, or thing, or ideal. We may, however, hope for a bit of clarity about the many configurations and maneuvers that affective attachments assume within human life.

1

Imagination

Imagination is funny; it makes a rainy day sunny. So the song goes. But it is out of that funniness that our reality evolves. We are both the product of this phenomenon and the creators of it. When I first began my investigations into the nature of love, my own imagination focused upon love as an imaginative theme in art, particularly literature. They seemed like an obvious target that my critical and philosophical arrow could not fail to reach at one place or another. The enterprise turned out to be endless in two respects. Not only was there a virtual infinity of works that deal with love but also I came to realize that imagination operates throughout the rest of life in multiple ways that resemble these fictional and often fanciful presentations. If love could be studied as imagination revealed in poetry and painting, sculpture and the opera, so too could life itself be approached as a template of the same imaginative processes that the various art forms use to articulate the nature and pursuit of love within their different media.

What then are these processes? In a book entitled *The Harmony of Nature and Spirit* I devoted a chapter to imagination in its relationship with idealization. I studied their function in the creation of meaning and as joint components within the human spirit. I now wish to extend that analysis by probing the role of both imagination and idealization in all affective attachments. In doing so, I may be able to augment our understanding of meaning, happiness, love, and the other elements of nature and spirit that I discussed.

In the book just mentioned I described imagination's preoccupation with possibles and with impossibles. The concept of possibility itself I left unexplored, and yet that is fundamental in this field of inquiry. It appears first, and most magnificently, in the Platonic doctrine of forms. All philosophers, not just logicians or rationalists of every stripe, must stand in awe of Plato's achievement. He taught us, as reflective creatures, how to view the world not only as a succession of actual objects, events, and experiential data that exist—that occur, both literally and unmistakably, in ordinary life—but also as the foreground for a plenitude of possibilities that may never be instantiated, may never be actualized, may never come into existence in any factual sense. To see the being of everything from this vantage point was to see a boundless panoply of qualities or properties that the human mind could entertain as constituents in a domain that only mind might truly fathom. The grandeur of the Platonic vision cannot be overemphasized. It exhilarates and takes one's breath away. Properly interpreted, it is the beginning of wisdom about our reality.

I believe that Plato did not interpret his doctrine properly. He thought of the mind as an a priori structure that has primarily two compartments. One contains intellect that is useful, indeed required, for coping with the environmental circumstances human beings must surmount in their attempt to satisfy organic needs. This practical reason enables us to survive in nature and to gratify our inclinations toward bodily pleasures or consummations. To have a good life, however, one had to know what goodness is, in itself and as a universal goal. Plato thought that this awareness depends on another kind of reason, in this connection worthy of being capitalized, as most translators have in order to signify its abstract character and metaphysical import. Through Reason of this sort the mind can presumably cut below the apparent surface of existence and find the meaning in everything that does exist.

Such meaningfulness, Plato maintained, is appreciated only by seeing how the actuality of something manifests and concretizes the mere possibility of there being anything that can be described as what it is. Through Reason one grasps the definition of general terms in ordinary language, and so the nature of whatever is sayable without logical contradiction. Reason thus displays the nature of mind itself as well as the objective order in the universe that mind is forever trying to comprehend.

I speak of this doctrine as a misinterpretation because it fails to recognize other components that are equally important in human cognition. Extrapolating beyond everyday reason as he does, Plato was himself using a type of imagination that enabled him even to conceive of possibility as something relevant to ultimate Reason. He was, moreover, a highly imaginative dramatic artist whose conversational writings are suitably called "dialogues."

The works of Plato are not cold or rigidly formal tracts, but rather vivid and richly speculative discussions. They are worthy of being treated as literature as well as philosophy. Yet Plato does little to analyze the nature of the imagination that was so native to him. He seems to have taken it for granted. He extols only Reason as a pipeline to the infinite possibilities that serve as preconditions for the world as we know it. He does not perceive that such objectivistic claims cannot be established by Reason itself. Indeed, if I am right, these claims illustrate how imagination—which has no pretensions of objectivity—struggles to make sense of the world we live in, to create a meaning for it whether or not reality embodies any independently.

This failure to recognize the importance of imagination led Plato into philosophical errors that the Western world has had to contend with ever since. The most glaring is the distinction between the two realms of being which Plato introduced as a matter of primal dogma. There was the world of appearance, present in sensory experience and accessible to practical reason, and there was the underlying and objective world that only Reason could apprehend. Until the nineteenth century, almost all of Western thought accepted this dualism as self-evident. The Romantics and the quasi-Romantic philosophers such as Hegel or Schelling sought to free themselves of many of its implications. But it was Nietzsche who first saw, clearly and with brilliant self-assurance, that this traditional view was inadmissible and had to be discarded entirely. Having been struck down before his intellectual growth could run its course, Nietzsche only intimated, but never fully developed, his belief that imagination is the key to showing how the older view may be transvalued by later philosophers.

In his working methodology Plato incorporates both the rationalist and the empiricist poles in his dualistic conception. While always relying upon his concept of a priori Reason, Plato also orients his thinking toward the ambiguities of ordinary experience. Not being systematic treatises, his dialogues rarely resolve anything, and they often end with confusion that is not unintended but rather proffered as heuristic inducement to reexamine the goals each dialogue has set itself. Though Socrates guides and dominates the exchange of ideas, he normally proceeds by imaginatively eliciting responses that were latent in his interlocutors. This is also true of the Socratic turn as it permeated, some two thousand years later, psychoanalytic therapy and collaterally the "method" type of acting taught by the Actor's Studio in New York.

Even at its most deductive, Socrates's method was interpersonal as well as rationalistic. He created logic as we know it, but he did so in the open, out-of-doors theater that the agora was. In the eighteenth century, Rousseau condemned the staged performances of his time because they occurred under artificial conditions and lacked the natural spontaneity of communal life. It is not surprising that Rousseau admired the content, and, more expressly, the setting of the Socratic dialogues as Plato reconstructs them.

What I find fascinating in these expositions of Socrates's talent is their attempt to discover abstract truths by formal means, such as *reductio ad absurdum*, that can alter anyone's thinking but only through a wizardry of direct, immediate, involvement that is neither deductive nor limited to logic. Though Socrates purported to be searching for conclusions that followed with necessity from undeniable premises, his art was based on a different kind of approach. In the *Meno* he shows his hand. Everyone knows what is real, he asserts in that dialogue, for we are all, and equally, immersed in reality. It surrounds and permeates everything we do or say. It is inescapable. If it is a problem for the intellect, that must result from our defective thinking about it. We cannot have an undistorted appreciation of reality because it is obscured by our imperfect reasoning. We therefore need a philosopher to purge our mental habits of cognitive impediments that are responsible for their malfunction.

This philosophic task is performed by the logic Socrates invents. But its benign intervention into human affairs, which is the ideal he followed and for which he was finally executed, results from an aesthetic and extralogical communication of the sort that Greek drama had always tried to institute. Socrates rightly thought that his mode of intellectual exploration was an artistic activity to which the cultivated youths of Athens could plausibly respond.

For his part, Plato treated the being of possibilities, the very *possibility* of possibility, as a beauty in itself. Though he was mistaken to assume that Reason unaided by imagination can detect a basic ontology of possibles, he was clear-headed in regarding possibility as a source of wonderment. Like Socrates, and like Socrates's other disciples, Plato was fully acquainted with the nature of actuality—with people, things, and ideals as they happen to exist in the world we experience as our own. Socrates had fought in battle, and Plato was later to be sold into slavery. The social and political upheavals related to Athenian imperialism, Spartan bellicosity, and the Peloponnesian War that erupted from their intersection were ever present in the consciousness of both thinkers. They were also familiar with Democritean and other materialist philosophies that preceded them. Like most Greeks having to endure their rocky shores and sweltering sun, they knew how unrelenting and recalcitrant nature could be.

The genius of the vision Plato formalized consisted in transcending the moment-by-moment intrusiveness of the actual by awareness of our human capacity to envisage possibilities not yet actualized. And even if they were never actualized, would they not retain their beauty as autonomous possibles? Like so many others, I feel grateful to Socrates and Plato for having revealed the splendor of this aesthetic vista discerned by them as something apart from the actual.

Plato argued that possibles belong to a realm of their own, a realm that is eternal. Everything that exists, perforce within the domain of actuality, could be interpreted as a sign or instantiation of some possibility, some form or essence that is timeless in itself because it cannot be reduced to the coordinates of time, or space, or anything else needed for existence. As long as it remains purely negative in this way, Plato's concept of eternity is innocuous. But by inferring that there must therefore be *another* reality, an independent and more fundamental being that sustains the apparent world, he committed a momentous non sequitur that would change the course of history. Perhaps because it was so astounding a travesty of our life in nature, it took humankind almost two millennia to detect the absurdity of its proclaimed dualism.

The guiding orientation of Platonic philosophy, whether in the ancient or the modern world, is untenable because it issues out of this dualism. Even Santayana, an exceptionally acute Neoplatonist of the twentieth century who understood the workings of imagination better than any of his forerunners, could not overcome the fractured outlook he inherited from Plato. That outlook was so arresting to the philosophic mind, and so satisfying as an object of aesthetic contemplation, that it prevented Platonists and Neoplatonists alike from constructing an acceptable theory about the very concept of possibility on which their entire doctrine rested. There are varied types of possibles, more than these philosophers generally considered. Until we specify the differences among them we cannot hope to explain how either Reason, as Plato thought, or imagination, as I do, can be operational not only in love but also in every other kind of affective attachment.

In his fixation on the deductive purity of Reason, the possibles that intrigued Plato most were those that fall into the category of "logical possibility." They are predicated upon a lack of self-contradiction and are exemplified by even the simplest tautology. That x equals x is indubitable. If we were to deny that something is what it is and not another thing, to paraphrase Bishop Butler, our cognitive faculty would disintegrate and we could not have reason of any sort. More enterprising truisms like "business is business" or "boys will be boys" go beyond mere logical possibility in two respects. First, they force us to consider whether some common assumptions, about the nature of business or of boyhood in my examples, may in fact be misleading. But then, they draw us back to themselves, as tautological certainties, with a sense that we have now tested and validated their truthfulness. Such uses of language can function in this fashion because definitions are linguistic markers for what shall henceforth be taken as the unquestionable meaning of a word or phrase. Definitions rule out self-contradiction in the range of discourse they establish, and to that extent they, too, belong to the category of logical possibility.

Plato was drawn to this bit of ontological taxonomy because it seemed to be an entrance into the only part of life that resists the ravages of temporal existence. "x equals x" is always true, whatever happens in time and space, and even if Heracleitus was right in thinking that everything that exists must change as a consequence of the fact that it does exist. Like Parmenides, Plato was searching for ways of uncovering a final reality that in itself would never change. Since Reason is the human mind organizing verities into valid patterns capable of generating inferences that are immune from existential uncertainties, only Reason could provide objective knowledge about reality. What Plato did not perceive or admit was the element of subjectivity already present in his system. The mentality that pounces on the absence of self-contradiction in a tautology is itself an effusion of human nature and therefore bound by the same limitations as all the rest of life in us.

Without truly understanding his discovery, Plato had stumbled upon one of the great mysteries that permeate our ontic state. We are finite creatures and yet our mind gives us a glimpse into something that seems to exceed all finite limits. Logical truths, even of the trivial type I have mentioned, have infinite scope. Nothing we can ever think of will ever gainsay them. It took a supreme genius like Plato to enunciate this. In applying his momentous insight, however, Plato failed to recognize that by itself rationality cannot do much with the self-consistencies it so greatly treasures. They had to be supplemented by a mental act that bestows importance upon the *manner* in which abstract possibility exceeds the purely factual. That segment of our being is not intellect or Reason, but rather imagination existing as a different albeit coherent faculty. Though Plato's own imagination was enormous, he did not see that *it* was finding what he thought he had discovered through his metaphysical science.

To distinguish a tautology from the brute actuality of some occurrence in nature is already an achievement of imagination. In being what it is, that occurrence acquires a quasi-certainty of its own. It *does* or *did* or *will* exist. Having experienced it, we cannot doubt that something has happened, even if we are unable to depict its inclusive reality with any accuracy. But imagination operates to free us from the restraints of this facticity. It does so merely by conceiving what is or is not logically possible within the format of our language. Plato seizes upon this elemental potency, focuses attention upon it, and revels in an engrossing discipline—as in mathematics or deductive argumentation—that results from our contemplating the abstract entities it filters out of our routine existence in time and space. The bestowal involved is not only imaginative in itself but also the means by which imagination enables us to make our crucial discrimination between the possible and the actual.

Only by reference to this human capability, and to the role of imagination in it, can we explain an affective attachment such as love. Having posited a domain that would encompass everything that is possible and therefore exempt from the finitude of temporality, Plato thought the inhabitants of that domain must all be universals. He concluded that authentic love would have to be directed toward them. He knew that things or persons or ideals occur as particulars, but he was convinced that this does not reveal why love is so important to human beings.

Throughout his analysis Plato underplays imagination and how it participates in love of any sort. He overlooks love's ability to emancipate us from the merely actual by emphasizing what is possible in it but not yet brought to its greatest potential. In having this attitude, we corroborate and sustain the individual being of the actuality that attracts us. Regardless of what it is and may become, we love it not by transferring our interest to a universality under which it can be subsumed but rather by accepting it in its own particularity. This is an act of imagination.

Though we cannot know what an object is unless we discern the universals that cooperate in its definition, our love for it is an imaginative bestowal of value upon its sheer specificity, its actual and possible attributes taken all together. In loving a person, a thing, or an ideal, we acknowledge and confirm its uniqueness. Universals are also unique, and they too may be loved. To do that, one has to be a philosopher perhaps, but the feat can be learned by those who are adequately trained. The Platonic philosopher, enamored of eternal forms, experiences a love that is meaningful to him. For most people, the requisite bestowal involves another type of imagination, one that is directed toward particulars but not the particularity of universals.

✳

Philosophers, especially those who were rationalists like Plato, may have neglected the service imagination provides because they conceived of it as a faculty that is *wholly* detached from intellect. This bifurcation continues in the modern assurance, still present at many universities, that science and the humanities belong to distinct and unrelated compartments with little or no effect upon each other. But the mind cannot live that way. It survives through what, in brain physiology, is called "mass action"—separate functions interacting and collaborating dynamically. Unless imagination operated in this fashion, we could have awareness of neither logical possibility nor of "empirical possibility," as I shall call it. Though quite different from each other, empirical and logical possibilities are complementarities. Science is a search for data and for theories that manifest what is possible in experience, empirically possible, but that must always exist within a context of logical possibility. Imagination is essential for both, and for the link between them.

The boundaries of empirical possibility are determined by what we (imaginatively) call "the laws of nature." Imagination enters into our use of this terminology since we have no evidence, no empirical basis, no rational or cognitive proof to sanction our belief that the cosmos is lawful throughout. The assumption that it is, and must be, derives from the backward abyss of theological mythology, which claimed that an anthropomorphic but all-powerful lawgiver laid down rules for nature to obey. In the primitive mentality of such conceptions, events that did not conform to these rules were deemed "unnatural." That was a way of saying that nature ought to obey, but sometimes defies, the laws that make it into what it really is.

So envisaged, the laws of nature were taken to be normative as well as metaphysical. They were like the regulations a judge might follow in adhering to some legal code that purports to reveal what is ethically obligatory. Though scientists may have outgrown their religious origins, many of them still cling to the assurance that there must be ultimate laws that determine what does or does not exist. Yet science keeps changing its ideas about the content of such laws. Its catalog of what is thought to be empirically possible and impossible often reflects developments in the sociology of scientific theorizing. Imagination plays a role in this, as it also does in the accumulation of evidential knowledge about the actualities themselves.

In comparable ways, imagination belongs to our awareness of all other types of possibility. Until recently, people thought it was "technically impossible" for human beings to travel faster than the speed of sound. But there was nothing in the laws of logic or of nature, nothing in logical or empirical possibility, to preclude the possibility of our achieving such higher velocities. We had only to acquire appropriate know-how and master the needed technology. Though that took time and professional dedication, the technical possibility for this—as for an endless number of other creative achievements—hovered in its own limbo for ages until it was actualized. At some moment in time, people got the "idea," as we say, that human beings can possibly move at great speed by mechanical means that even surpass the flight of birds.

Without a Leonardo da Vinci this technical possibility might never have arisen in our species. But once the thought occurred, finding expression in Leonardo's drawings and the speculation of others, it could steadily evolve throughout the following centuries. The years that intervened between the originating conception and the final attainment, between the dream of mechanized transport and its eventual realization, is a history of expanding imagination as well as intellectual progress.

I will not try to analyze or even enumerate all types of possibility. For my purposes it will be enough to mention just one more, itself a cluster of several others. I am thinking of what I call "practical or moral possibility." In a vital situation demanding a reaction to a thing, a person, or an ideal that directly concerns us, we are faced by a need to choose among available possibilities. In the Danny Kaye film *Me and the Colonel*, adapted from the Franz Werfel play *Jacobowsky and the Colonel*, a resourceful Jewish tailor saves the life of a proud, aristocratic Polish officer during the Nazi invasion by acting on the principle that "there are always two possibilities." That numerical detail accentuates the drama and the humor of their efforts to stay alive, but in his heart the tailor must have known that there are always a great number of alternate possibilities. He has trouble helping the colonel escape their enemies because the nobleman can admit only one possibility—whatever his strict code of honor and fidelity demands under the circumstances. Only that registers on him as a moral necessity, and therefore nothing else matters to him. For *him* there can be no other practical possibility.

In taking this stance, which he begins to alter when he surmises that the tailor's system of values may often be superior to his own, the colonel has used his imagination to eliminate all modes of response other than those that fit the class and status to which he was born. We might say that imagination in him precludes the wider and more flexible disposition that the tailor maintains in order to outwit forces that are intent upon destroying persons like himself. Even though their use of it is radically different, imagination exists as a creative principle in both the colonel and the tailor. For each of them it is instrumental in deciding what shall count as an acceptable, and in that sense valid, possibility.

On the other hand, one could argue that the colonel's kind of mentality shows a lack of imagination, for he limits his conduct to a single range of possibles. Yet that limitation also has its imaginative scope. It may not prolong his life or even further the mission he wants to serve, but it is geared to the possibility of consecutive self-sacrifice that means more to him than anything else. His devotion is worthy of respect, even admiration. The tailor's cleverness in preserving himself and those he cares about, including the colonel, is also something we admire. In him we applaud the efficacy and versatility of his imagination. A latter-day Figaro or Sancho Panza, he manipulates real and persistent difficulties of life through his inspired alertness to one practical possibility after another.

In its variable occurrence, imagination enables the colonel and the tailor to have their different orientations, and it is only by reference to imagination as it exists in anyone that we can understand why some mode of behavior is morally and emotionally possible to that person while other responses are not.

These examples of types of possibility as they are present to imagination can provide us with new vistas about the nature of feeling. Through love we accept a person, a thing, or an ideal as it is in itself, as just the particularity that it is, as the unique entity it has become. To enact this acceptance, we must entertain the logical possibility of its never having existed. Yet there it is, an actuality that fills our consciousness day and night. Much of the wonderment of love arises from this intuition. By accepting the object, however, we dislodge it from its status as *mere* actuality. We affirm its being, not in thinking it should remain unchanged in all respects but rather in committing ourselves to it, as what it is and despite the faults or blemishes it undoubtedly has. We *con*firm its existence, side *with* it, treat it as something whose value and importance are logical possibilities worth sustaining in the actual world, which, being actual, is always capable of obliterating them. Imagination is needed for us to assume a posture such as this. Without it there would be no valuation at all, only an awareness of facts that occur as brute events in space and time.

In this fashion imagination serves as a prerequisite for love. But imagination also has an additional role in it. Accepting the beloved as is, the lover must have some conception of empirical possibilities and impossibilities that pertain to what that person is or is not. They specify the conditions under which he or she can even exist.

When Heidegger speaks of death as the everpresent possibility of impossibility, he must be referring to what is empirically possible, and he is right insofar as death is the natural occurrence that consists in our being eliminated from the class of actualities. To remain actual as a human being is to retain those empirical possibilities without which there cannot be life rather than death. The abolition of these possibles is what lovers fear, not only for themselves, as all people do, but also because it can happen to the beloved and thereby undermine the meaningfulness of the lover's life. Through imagination enflamed by love's ardent fixation upon the being of the beloved, the lover will often suffer greater distress at the prospect of the other's demise than at the imminence of the one that he or she must also experience.

We all know that we will die someday and most of us give little thought to this fatality. But the idea that the beloved might die is often unbearable to a lover who cannot imagine how one can go on living after that catastrophe. This possibility boggles an imagination that expends much of its energy on the continued presence of a single object. Love gives meaning to a person's life by devoting itself to the viability of life in someone else. When that other life is destroyed, one's own survival may seem to be a pointless possibility that defeats the authenticity of the love one had.

Of course, friends and counselors can try to revitalize or enlarge the lover's imagination by reminding him or her of all the other people who may now be loved, and all the other avenues of beauty or goodness that still remain in nature. In doing so, the well-wishers move beyond what is logically, empirically, or technically possible or impossible. They engage the element of practical possibility as the one that has the greatest immediacy in whatever attachment human beings are able to experience. The death of the beloved is a crushing blow not because the lover fears the world will be extinguished once that event occurs, but rather because he or she cannot imagine ever *wanting* to exist in such a world. The idea of pursuing normal interests in it seems wholly vapid. The meaning of the lover's life having been uprooted, if not destroyed, under the altered conditions that death entails, how can there persist anything that has vital or moral importance for the lover? "How could I seek the empty world again?", as Emily Brontë puts it in her poem "Remembrance."

Since love—like every affective attachment—exists at different intensities and in different degrees of dependency, what I have just described may seem extreme. Even so, it reveals how imagination, and the kind of possibility I am designating as practical or moral, functions in all or many instances of love. Throughout my earlier speculations, I characterized love as an expression of imagination impinging upon the purposive layers of our existence. Purposiveness shows forth the appraisive type of valuation that judges what an object is worth to us either individually or objectively. As a branch of inductive science, appraisal assesses the value something has in being that which satisfies our needs and desires, or else the needs and desires of some valuational community that represents society at large.

I saw bestowal as a supplement to appraisal, a compensation for it, and even, in its own manner, a liberation from it. I claimed that without bestowal of value there would be no love—at least, not as we have defined it in the Western world, and in recent centuries throughout most other cultures as well. To elucidate the nature of bestowal, I described imagination as that which allows human beings to create in themselves an ability to transcend, and so to modify, their appraisive inclinations. The view I am now proposing amplifies this line of reasoning.

If one associates love with imagination that awakens active and emotional interests perceived as moral possibilities, one has to emphasize the affective price that men and women pay in thus allowing themselves to bestow value over and above the appraisal of it. The expansiveness of imagination required for bestowal to exist generates its own diminution in other ways. This happens not only when the beloved dies or is lost, or when the lover anticipates that one and possibly both of these eventualities will occur at some time in the near future, but also in every moment that love is alive and consummatory.

That is why we treat as quite authentic the image of lovers peering into each other's eyes, or holding hands while they march forward to a single destiny, or joining their bodies in sexual intercourse that may be a spiritual oneness as well as a material embrace. All these amatory acts signify that the lovers permit no other emotional and practical possibilities to intrude upon the exceptional meaning that they find and create in each other. By establishing the interpersonal dedication they feel, the imagination in both of them systematically curtails these other possibilities in order to favor the ones that have been chosen as the mainstay of their present bestowals. This is a price many people are willing to pay, though the cost is often very high.

❄

My initial statement of the distinction between bestowal and appraisal took the form it did because of the long history of works in philosophy, literature, and other arts that deal with the nature of love. They were produced by imagination as a creative agency that acquires a quasi-autonomous role in the human mind. Various theorists had even claimed that love differs from other aspects of our life in being illusory, irrational, fragile, ethereal, not-of-this-world, and perhaps attainable *only* in imagination. But few of these less than completely desirable properties were adequately analyzed by any of the commentators, and no one succeeded in showing how the condition they depicted could be either liberating or creative.

Though the realists had their doubts, many of the idealists affirmed that love is either the *summum bonum* or, at least, the best that human beings can hope for on earth. In my own approach, I suggested that we study the different modes of imagination that love employs in daily life as well as in art and philosophy. For this endeavor to succeed, one had to remain faithful to the fact that, exhilarating as imagination can be, it is sometimes ridiculous or conceptually suspect. We could then avoid the unwarranted ascriptions of both realists and idealists. Together with the concept of idealization that I employed, I hoped that my pluralistic views about imagination would suffice.

In time I realized how much more must be said. Imagination is an incursion upon the world. It is a revision that may not change the way things are but can nevertheless affect the way we experience or *en*visage them. When critics of mine, Russell Vannoy, for instance, interpreted my idea of bestowal as "subjectivistic," they claimed I ignored the traits of the beloved that are desirable apart from any values projected by a lover's imagination. In later writings I tried to answer such objections.[1] But only now do I perceive that an adequate reply necessitates a more comprehensive theory of imagination than any I had as yet provided.

In undertaking that task, I begin by noting how greatly imagination, as the illuminating of possibilities, invests all human consciousness—not just the experience of love (or any other affect). As a first approximation in this chapter, I distinguished the possible from the actual. But the two are forever interwoven; they constantly interact in even the most pedestrian moments of purposive existence or given factuality. The stone we trip on is something else as well. It is a temporal interference in our path through life, a deterrent to our progress, an assault upon our freedom and will to power. Getting past it, we look back instinctively, partly to locate its position so that we can avoid it in the future but also to assert through mere perception our intellectual supremacy over it. We treat it as if it were a person whom we fixate with our stare, in that way assuring ourselves that its brief triumph has no lasting importance.

Our response is part of our equilibration with an actuality that confronts us—this particular stone having caused us to stumble or fall. We transform it into a significant entity in our experience, and thereby confirm our own autonomous being. That reaction divests the event of any permanent domination over us. We are able to do this because imagination is always invoking present and future possibles that transcend the actual. In extraordinary cases, an actuality might seem to be a pristine datum unencumbered by any reverberating possibilities. But in virtually all of life—which is to say, circumstances as they ordinarily occur—there are no pristine data.

Having said this, I am reminded of a television interview with the film director William Wyler. At one point he discusses the making of his movie *The Heiress*. In the scene in which Ralph Richardson returns home late at night and discovers Olivia de Havilland asleep on the settee in the hall of their house, we see Richardson open the front door and enter. Wyler was famous for not giving acting advice to his performers, though he forced them to go through take after take until he got what he was looking for. He reports that on this occasion Richardson asked him how he would like him to play the scene. Wyler answered, with surprise at the question, that there were not many ways of doing it. But he then remarks: "He showed me about, I don't know, eight or eleven ways, and it was like a symphony each time, and so effortless, and each one a little different."[2]

Wyler tells this anecdote to illustrate the greatness of Richardson as an actor. But it also reveals what happens throughout human consciousness, and above all in our affective response to things, persons, and ideals that matter to us. The phenomenon is especially prominent in relations of love, but it belongs to all other forms of attachment as well. They each employ imaginative bestowals of value that enable us to make the world meaningful for ourselves. To some degree, and with varying talent, human beings are generically actors of the sort that Ralph Richardson was superlatively.

All the same, we may still wonder how bestowal of value can be distinguished from appraisal. Vannoy, like other philosophers in the past, believes that love always reduces to an estimation of what the object of desire is worth appraisively in relation to one's own interests and apart from any intrusion by creative imagining. If Vannoy is right, love must be considered a search for "objective," rather than "subjective," value. In order to assert, as I do, that love is not objective in this sense, since acts of amatory imagination inevitably change our relation to the object, we must prove that bestowal may exist as a contributing principle. Unless it does, it can scarcely belong to the definition of love, and Vannoy's critique would then be justified.

The key to the needed explication lies in my assumption, which might well be unverifiable, that in itself every actuality is a unique and irreducible particular, ontologically indefeasible as such. But if we cannot reduce an actual to any categories or modes of generalization that our intellect employs in order to make sense of it, how can we know what it is? If we argue that an actuality may be experienced in its mere concreteness, do we not forfeit our ability to give it a name, to classify it with similar or different objects and events, or even to claim that what we take to be imagination belongs to any awareness of it? We would seem to have put ourselves into a speculative impasse.

We avoid this consequence by further analyzing the nature of each being's individuality. In appreciating that all experience is what it is by virtue of possibilities present to someone's imagination as well as through its being a factuality that occurs in time and space, we perceive that knowing about an object means recognition of how actuals and possibles converge at every moment. From the very outset, I have emphasized that love arises from a mixture of appraisal and bestowal. This new formulation allows me to say that even when appraisal harkens to a given objectivity of value, that itself involves bestowal as a responsive acceptance of desired possibilities proffered through our everworking imagination. The element of bestowal in love must therefore be an extension or elaboration of something that is already present in our experience of the actual. Bestowal is operative within the possibilities that bring appraisal into existence, possibilities without which there could be no appraisal. Bestowal will still be seen to depend on imagination, but now we can affirm that both participate in appraisiveness itself.

Even in my earliest writing I spoke of bestowal as an imaginative and creative act. I described it as affirmative acceptance of the object as it is, whatever it may be in time and space. I saw it as entailing the fabrication of a new relationship through which the mere identity of an object could be confirmed and also enjoyed. This interactive event, this emergent complex of practical possibilities, was therefore to be understood as a sustaining response, a commitment to the object in itself, that issues out of the lover's imagination. I portrayed love as gratuitous, freely offered, because no wholly appraisive evaluation could ever account for it.

My subsequent explorations into different types of bestowal and the ideals or idealizations by which they affect moral, social, and political actualities were designed to demonstrate how the search for love enters into human experience as well as into the structure of philosophical theories about the nature of love. This led me to study the affective quest as it progressively tries to find and create meaning through our different ways of loving persons, things, and ideals. A complete understanding of such creativity was not attempted, though chapters on the relations between imagination, idealization, and the aesthetic sought to clear a bit of the wilderness.

What still lies before us is the need to show how imagination functions as an intermeshing of possibles and actuals that comprise our value-laden experience of the world. This happens in love but also in sexuality, in compassion, in friendliness, and throughout the other colorations in the spectrum of our attachments. Each constitutes a linkage between some play of imagination and the active feelings, desires, emotions—in short, the organic springs of our affective being—that exist as propellant forces in human motivation. Art is especially attuned to these realities because the aesthetic element in life is closely allied to imagination (and idealization), and to the attainment of consummations for which feeling always hungers. To see this with any precision, however, we must carry the argument into aspects of imagination that have not yet been discussed.

One thing that immediately comes to mind is the fact that imagination is *innovative*. Through it we seek to renew ourselves and change the world. But are we truly capable of doing either? Some philosophers would claim we are not, and their reasoning may have some merit. In moving beyond the facticity of our experience, in freeing ourselves from the actual, transcending it insofar as we conceive of alternative possibilities, do we ever attain more than just a reshuffling of what already has existed? In imagining some uninstantiated possible—let us say, a flying space machine that approaches the speed of light—are we not constructing in the mind a revision of actualities we have encountered thus far, changing them only in the superficial sense that they are now used to picture some realignment of their own components?

If we do say this, we take an unduly modest attitude toward the creativity in human life, or in the world. It is a view that comports well with the determinism, reductivism, and parsimony of intellectual baggage that many scientists think essential for their expertise. As metaphysics, their perspective may be neither more nor less justifiable than any other. I myself find it barren and contrary to my own sense of reality. I am recurrently astonished by the variability of life. I perceive it as always originating developments that point in diverse directions, achieving or being defeated by results that may well be unforeseeable. I have no hesitation in believing that the universe is a succession of changes that are authentically novel, irreducible to anything else, and normally in process of unbounded evolution that has to be accepted as a given in the cosmos as we know it.

Since this would apply to faculties of spirit as well as particles of material substance, we may well affirm that the innovations presented to our consciousness by imagination are indeed new possibles and not just a reheating of ontological dishes we have been served time and again in the past. Critics might assert that such opinions recommend themselves because it is so flattering to think that our ability to imagine fresh possibilities bespeaks a creativity that would not exist apart from this alleged power in us. But even if my belief assumes a virtue though we have it not, life goes on in our species as it does only because most human beings have some faith of that sort. I therefore feel no need to vindicate my acquiescence in the idea that imagination helps germinate realities over and above the ones that might occur otherwise.

Without the innovative aspect of imagination, affective experience could not exist. Being commonplace creatures in the world of nature, we relate to each other as unavoidable factualities. As Heidegger puts it, the being to which we are born and henceforth live is one into which we are thrown (*geworfen*), tossed haphazardly. The world of our existence is just there, and since it largely consists of other people, we must learn how to deal with them as the actual men and women that they are. If they can satisfy our needs and desires, we welcome them as contributors to our experience who enact this beneficial gratuity. If they threaten us, or wish to treat us as potentialities for their own satisfaction under conditions that are unfavorable to ourselves, we ward them off as best we can. Imagination pervades this interaction with reality. It gives birth to innovations that foster one or another kind of affective attachment (or detachment).

As a disposition that accepts an object in itself, love cannot be just a self-serving attempt to bring it closer to one's heart's desire. That would be a strictly appraisive attitude, which consequently lacks the kind of bestowal needed for love. The innovations that bestowal institutes are ways of accepting the object as is, and despite its negative attributes. In the process, bestowal alters our experience of the object through imaginative devices that define some modality of positive feeling. Negative attitudes rely upon other innovations that imagination also proffers.

These panoramic statements may seem paradoxical at first, but any sense of inconsistency dissolves once we remember the differences between bestowal and appraisal. The innovations that bestowal creates are changes primarily in oneself, and not necessarily in the object. The blemish in the other person's appearance becomes a treasure, even a beauty, to the lover because it is no longer perceived as something to be evaluated in the appraisive mode alone. Its value has been bestowed upon it by the lover's acceptance of the beloved, which involves acceptance of various data: their relationship as what it is, the autonomous being of the other person which continues to exist independently of their bond, the sharing of themselves that causes each to identify with the other's search for personal welfare.

All this issues from the capacity for bestowing value that human beings, and other animals as well, have access to as part of their nature. We are born to this innovative capacity, or acquire it at a very early stage of maturation, and it persists throughout our lives as a principal means by which we make the world meaningful to ourselves.

To say that basically the innovations of love occur in the lover rather than the beloved is not, however, entirely accurate. Though these innovations come into being through the imaginative responses of the lover, they take on a reality that neither lover nor beloved can have separately. That is most striking when there is mutual love, each person then being simultaneously the lover and the beloved of the other. Bestowing value upon a man or woman who bestows it upon oneself, the two people in this interpersonal type of love may no longer be able to demarcate what they are as individuals, or would want appraisively if they were pulled apart. They have remade themselves in terms of their relationship and their commitment to that relationship. The resulting innovations create values that mutually affect each of them, and both reciprocally, as if the tie between them had a life of its own.

We know, of course, that it does not. Only the human beings involved, as particular persons, can engender the requisite imagination that makes possible these innovative bestowals. Each of them must also endure any pain or failure that accompanies their perilous attempt to find meaning through love. Once love occurs, both will undergo transformations that may or may not be to the ultimate advantage of either. Whatever may eventuate, the lovers are responsible. They cannot escape the fact that life, in them as in everyone else, is always subject to appraisive considerations that must occur throughout. Pure bestowal does not exist.

Nor does pure appraisal. These forms of valuation exist in a ricochet between the two of them. Neither is reducible to the other. In all affective life they intersect unceasingly, though often unnoticed. They depend on the innovative capacity of imagination as the source not only of changes people create in the world at large but also of modifications in oneself. Bestowal controls our desire to use other things, persons, or ideals for reasons of our own; appraisal regulates the purposive responses without which we could not bestow at all. In a later phase, appraisal turns back upon the values that come out of bestowal and decides whether they are ethically or socially defensible from its own, appraisive, point of view at that level.

Since there is no guarantee that any love will be moral or even justifiable, love is ordinarily dangerous. Beautiful as it may be, it can prove disastrous to all involved, even criminal and outright evil. Being an emergent unity of bestowal and appraisal under conditions that have their own unique particularity, the existence of love is and must be subject to negative as well as positive appraisals and bestowals as they interact with each other in all further circumstances.

The innovative character of imagination has been increasingly recognized throughout the history of psychiatric theory. Though some writers maintain, in the words of one analyst, that "all finding is refinding," many professionals know that this is only a half-truth.[3] Time being unidirectional, the present must originate in the past; but what is found and taken as evidence of the past generally reflects an element of creativity in the refinding itself. Even Freud's tenacious determinism was shaken when he realized that what his patients reported about their early lives were often falsehoods or imaginative, though significant, distortions in their memory. We make the past meaningful by re-creating it from our present point of view, and that point of view becomes meaningful as the basis for later re-creations. Nothing is refound as a detachable nugget plucked out of the swampy mire of the past.

In trying to help a patient cope with deeply rooted problems, the therapist keeps in mind the individual continuity of ongoing innovations. Without discussing the aesthetics in this situation, he or she directs the patient's imagination into avenues of fruitful searching and problem solving. Successful as this joint effort may be, the outcome is sure to be uncertain. Novelty is always hard to predict. Transference love itself is a tentative effort by the patient to discover a meaning in some previous period of life by re-animating its ingredient feelings and directing them toward the therapist. The impulse that motivates this attachment may be related to what it was many years before, as addressed to one's mother or father perhaps, but the tactic can be helpful only if the patient appreciates the inventiveness in it. Such innovation is essential for competence in any art, including the art of living a good life. The ability of imagination to change our affective world through innovative re-creations gives it the power to alleviate (and also to cause) moral distress, and to cure as well as foster mental illness.

❋

While these ideas about possibility and innovation as components of imagination may help explain the nature of affective attachment, they must be seen in relation to a region of the human mind that I've not yet broached in this chapter. In two recent books I've described a province of imagination that I call "the imaginary." As an attempt to analyze the nature of art, and fiction as a whole, my speculation about the imaginary furthered my thinking about aesthetic foundations of the human spirit. Since our pursuit of love, and of other modes of attachment, results in values that reveal what we mean by spirit, much of what I had to say about the imaginary applies to affect itself. But what I offered was only a blueprint, and now I wish to map their relation more completely.

In its role within imagination, the imaginary is typically and distinctively human. It requires an intellectual capacity that exceeds the mental equipment of all other creatures on earth. Some of our fellow participants in animate existence may very well have imagination not entirely different from ours. A dog who sees his master put on an overcoat will make preliminary movements as if he thinks it is quite possible the two of them may be going for a walk. The dog could be said to "entertain" this and other possibilities, to keep them "in mind." But we have no reason to think that he has a *concept* of possibility.

Since human beings do, we can infer that they also have concepts of impossibility. But are ideas of possible and impossible polarities of each other? Can we imagine an impossibility, a negative possible, exactly as we imagine possibilities? This question takes us directly into reflection about the imaginary. While we know that the conjunction of x and not-x is impossible, nothing being able to be both itself and not itself, we may wonder what it is like to *imagine* that impossibility. Would it not mean treating it as a possibility, which is self-contradictory? In principle we can imagine any possible, regardless of how far it goes beyond the actual. That is basic in the mere having of imagination. Imagining a negative possible would necessitate an additional mental act. If impossibilities can be encompassed by imagination, that must be analyzed as a special case.

My conception of the imaginary tries to show what is distinctive in the imagining of negative possibilities. I view our imagination as versatile enough to include utterances that are self-contradictory, and therefore meaningless to that extent. Saying, for instance, that one is oneself and not oneself makes no sense at all, assuming that we are not equivocating in the use of the crucial terms. Yet we frequently communicate through this and similar locutions as if they had a meaning of their own, a meaning that other persons can understand through recognized forms of language. When people speak "poetically," whether or not they are poets, they often make statements that are nonsensical as literal discourse but are meaningful all the same. What is sensically conveyed is a general feeling about the matter at hand, a feeling that obliquely expresses a wide range of feelings or emotions that someone may experience. This capability derives from imagination and, above all, from the process that defines the imaginary.

Confronted by a remark that even the enormous spectrum of possibilities cannot explicate, the imaginary looks for a meaning that may be elicited from the linguistic or experiential setting of the statement. Asked how he feels this morning, the man who replies that he is not himself today is telling us something we seem to understand. Nevertheless, we are baffled if we search for a literal meaning. What else besides himself could he be? As a viable tactic, imagination might view the man as possibly meaning that he is not well. Generally he feels fine in the morning, but it is possible that this day he has the flu and so the world of his experience takes on a different aura to him. Or perhaps he wants us to know that he is traveling incognito: he thus pretends to be a person he is not. We comprehend this use of language because ordinary aspects of imagination are well equipped to handle it. But if we are informed that the man means nothing that lends itself to any such interpretations, the imaginary takes over and seeks another type of meaning.

Having eliminated the usual possibilities, the imaginary asks why anyone would make an assertion that is so obviously inconsistent. What is there in this man's circumstance, as one who seems to be expressing something about his personal experience, that leads him to talk in that manner? If he wanted us to know that he is not well, and therefore does not feel this morning as he almost always does, he could have said so explicitly. But what is said explicitly binds itself to the limitations of its own explicitness. It does not encourage chromatic excursions beyond the obvious, or into layers of possible significance that the speaker himself may not fully recognize.

Scanning these obscure and sometimes hidden meanings, the imaginary chooses those that may be appropriate in the current communication. It puts them into a coherent configuration of positive possibilities, and thus adapts them to more prosaic uses of imagination. The man in question is taken to mean not that he is literally not himself but rather that his present feelings are uncommon to him, foreign to his nature, so uncharacteristic of his mere identity as to be impossible in that sense.

This indirect, even devious activity of imagination is the imaginary using figurative language. That can be very appropriate for telling a story and creating a mood. It enables a fictional representation to captivate the listener's own imagination. Even though the distillated possibles may correspond to some actuality—the man really does feel what he claims to be feeling—his experience has been conveyed through a technique that reaches the actual by invoking blatant impossibilities that force us to envisage, through imagination, complicated realities that might ordinarily have been inaccessible. These could have been suggested or implied by a factual proposition, but then there would have been a more constrictive boundary for the intended meanings than one gets by stimulating our imaginative faculty to its maximum.

Why should one want this greater extensiveness? Because life itself has no fixed or sharply demarcated limits. We do not, and cannot, know what we are exactly, or what we are capable of doing and feeling under all conditions, or even what we are truly feeling at any given time. Since we have in general so little knowledge about the actualities of our immediate being, we invent scenarios for ourselves that are fictive and inherently nonverifiable. Through them as they are formulated by the imaginary, and hence by imagination in its widest application, we fabricate a portrayal of what we take to be ourselves and of the world as we live in it. Though this kind of discourse may not be literally true, or even logically consistent, it issues into a metaphoric presentation of our reality.

These fictional imaginings come to us spontaneously and most often without deliberation. They are ever active in our daily life. They result from material, physiological, occurrences of which we are usually unaware. Though partly dependent on our sensory equipment, they are not reducible to visual or auditory images, or to any other specifiable sensations. When the imaginary produces a make-believe that is sufficiently persuasive, we may deem its product truthful to the world we know. But this cannot be the kind of truth that science pursues. Scientific truth also uses imagination as a tool within its enterprise, but it normally eschews the imaginary as fictional in the sense of being illusory, or else as too ambiguous and amorphous to be reliable. For *aesthetic* truth, however, the imaginary's capacity to innovate without restraint is quite acceptable and no deterrent. Nor is it limited to what is narrowly called art. It has an important function throughout affective life as a whole. Every type of attachment depends on it—love, as so many poets reveal, and sex, friendship, compassion, or any other bond.

❄

In some respects my ideas about the imaginary as a region of imagination resemble those of both Wittgenstein and Sartre. In his own way, each rejected, as I do, the empiricist philosophies of the eighteenth century which reduced our imagination to the experience of images, themselves considered to be only diminished replicas of sensations ("impressions," as Hume called them). Wittgenstein emphasized the difference between imagination and the having of either sensations or simple imagery. When he said that earlier thinkers were misled by a picture, he meant (among other things) that imagination is not an inspecting of visual mental objects similar to the viewing of those that appear in perception. Wittgenstein speaks of imagining as simulating, playing a role, acting as if, pretending what it is like to have some experience, rather than being a duplication of some perceptual content in it.[4] Gilbert Ryle carries this approach further when he points out that pretending, and imagination as a whole, is an enactment in make-believe of what one knows. In that sense, Ryle suggests, "there is no special Faculty of Imagination, occupying itself single-mindedly in fancied viewings and hearings."[5]

For his part, Sartre identifies imagination with the imaginary as he conceives of it and then argues that the imaginary and the perceptual are "irreconcilable." In his book *L'imaginaire: psychologie phénoménologique de l'imagination*, Sartre claims that imagination is of "the unreal," its contents being nothing in the real world and therefore belonging to the ontological domain of nothingness rather than reality.[6] In effect, this notion reduces all imagination to the part of it that I have been calling the imaginary. Because the imaginary treats impossibilities as if they were indeed possible, as I have been saying, one might describe it as an excursion into Sartre's poetico-philosophical realm of nothingness and the unreal. But though the imaginary is essential for the existence of fiction or make-believe, Sartre fails to recognize that it differs from other segments of imagination. These nonimaginary elements in ordinary imagination concern themselves with possibles that are far from being unreal nothings. They are not predicated upon logical inconsistencies, as the imaginary is, and they serve as integral components within all perceptual awareness of the world. Most of human consciousness relies upon their interpenetration with actualities that we experience as themselves the embodiment of one or another possibility. Since the result of this interpenetration is neither nothing nor unreal, the positive possibilities in imagination cannot be characterized as Sartre renders them.

In an attempt to get beyond the difficulties in Sartre's formulation, Edward S. Casey defines imagination in terms of "pure possibility." He says: "By 'pure possibility' is meant a kind of possibility that is posited and contemplated *for its own sake* and not for the sake of anything external to, or more ultimate than, itself. . . . Consequently, pure possibility is the distinctive thetic character of what we imagine, and as such it serves to distinguish imaginative experience from other kinds of experience."[7] But the only possibility that can be contemplated for its own sake is logical possibility. All other types impinge upon some empirical or technical or moral actuality that can be their instantiation. They are as distinctively a part of human imagination as the one that Casey singles out. As for the imaginary, whose negative possibilities cannot be contemplated in the manner that Casey intends, it has in relation to affective attachment a special importance beyond any positive possibilities—particularly those that can be designated as "pure."[8]

❄

The imaginary effects of imagination appear most obviously within the bestowals that contribute to interpersonal love. Existing as we do, each of us may be considered just a class of empirical data that comprise our individuality. However much a mother dotes upon her child, she must accommodate herself to the fact that this offspring of herself is not an angel or gift from heaven, but instead a small animal driven by organic motors. It is subject, from moment to moment and in all future development, to needs and self-maintaining interests of its own. It is capable of someday becoming evil as well as good, and must be molded by social and ethical mandates that will serve as a virtual second nature to it.

These contingencies, which science may study with great success, can nevertheless be encased within a corroborative and affirmative attitude that constitutes the mother's love for this child. Though it is a distinct, indeed autonomous, creature that was once a part of her body but is no more, she may continue to identify with it for the rest of her life. Her sense of oneness is more than just a cognitive recognition of the facts in this situation. It is an affective nexus of feelings, emotional responses that reverberate between her child and herself as the mother of this person. These manifest the evolving imagination that exists in both, and that may persist as a meaningful determinant within their relationship. But what is the nature of this determinant? As an interpersonal attachment, it is a projection, a construction, an imaginary work of art. It is a living fiction the two create collectively for themselves.

Bestowal enacts this fiction, which attains value by means of it and beyond any satisfaction of purposive needs. Bestowing value upon a thing, a person, or an ideal, we augment the being of the other and attain a meaningful life for ourselves. The fiction then becomes a sustaining actuality. Our sustenance occurs within the innovative possibilities of a bond that defines what we shall feel and do and believe.

Since appraisal entails some prior search for organic satisfaction, feelings engendered by the bestowal of value may or may not be justifiable with respect to appraisive goodness. They can often be erroneous, unwarranted, illusory, treacherous in various ways. That is why cynical philosophers are prone to insist that love is deceptive. What they neglect is the more important fact that bestowal resorts to affirmations that are logically different from what these philosophers presuppose. Bestowal issues into affective declarations that are not inherently factual. They *alter* human actualities, making them conform to the imagined reality of what we have chosen to accept. In contrast to the overt representations that appraisal invokes, the expressiveness in bestowal is generally self-fulfilling prophecy. It occurs before, or at least apart from, the actualities that may eventually change enough to make it credible. Though equally authentic, the truthfulness of love must therefore be unlike anything that science or appraisive valuation can encompass.

In having this peculiar potency, interpersonal love may achieve the kind of aesthetic truth that all fine arts aspire toward. The imaginary aspect of imagination is the agency for this kind of truthfulness. It emancipates spirit from the meager confines of material nature. It shows us what there is in life that makes the creation of meaning and of value the groundwork for consummatory experience. If we could exist at a totally cognitive level, and as beings who have perfect powers of reason and deduction, there would be no need for the imaginary. But we are not beings of that sort.

Not only are we of imagination all compact, as Theseus in Shakespeare's *A Midsummer Night's Dream* says about the lunatic, the lover, and the poet, but also we are composed of feelings and nonideational inclinations too minute and finely woven for cognition to comprehend or analyze as it would like. Aesthetic truth, when it exists, gives us immediate awareness of the affective and imaginative elements in our being. We intuit, not infer, the range of possibles and impossibles that are available to consciousness. We treat them not as external and quantifiable bits of existence, but rather as qualities present in all experience though highly diversified. These instantiated possibles take on meaning in accordance with our sense of reality, our feeling about the world that is real *for* us, and for our persistent intimation, however vague, that much of it depends upon unformulatable sentiments as opposed to any clear and distinct ideas.

Being the human aptitude that employs the affectivity in bestowal as a means of reacting against, and compensating for, the demands of purposive appraisal, love reveals how thoroughly the imaginary saturates our appetitive and consummatory responses. Since appraisal and bestowal cannot be totally independent of each other, or understood apart from the multiple connections between them, we may well conclude that the imaginary within imagination occurs, to some degree, in all types of affective attachment. It, like them, should not be considered the falsification of anything. Nor is it just a conglomerate of learned reactions that one or another society has favored in the course of history. It is a fundamental part of human nature.

2

Idealization

For a fuller understanding of imagination, we need to consider how it is related to idealization.[1] Though Plato ignored the role of imagination in his official theories about love, he made the concept of idealization a basic pillar in his philosophic edifice. Having aligned himself with the rationalistic approach, however, Plato misconstrued the vital dimensions of idealization: he thought of it as mainly cognitive and scarcely dependent upon feeling or imagination. As against his view, I argue that the interpenetration between idealization and imagination is crucial in the being of each, and that their unity appears throughout our search for affective attachments as well as in our experience of them.

Plato's mistake in disprizing imagination for the sake of advocating idealization that reason favors is compounded by another that also warrants examination. Viewing love from an idealistic perspective, Plato believed that it alone reveals the ultimate nature of idealization. Affective dispositions of a different kind he treated as products of a natural, even material, condition that human beings undergo insofar as they belong to the lower world of appearance. Since this inferior realm also yearns for the ideality of what is good and beautiful, Plato portrays it as a restless but unavailing quest for the realities that idealization seeks. Appearance could have no final ideality and, possibly, no goodness at all. It was nothing but the brute fundament that idealization transcends just as true love does. In itself, appearance could only be a futile hunger for some purifying consummation that is nonphysical and therefore lies beyond it.

This ambivalent conception, typical of Plato's philosophy, pervades his ideas about sexuality. In *The Symposium* Socrates tells us that sex is a natural drive that girls and boys should be taught to accept as a proper and normal part of maturation in everyone. They should also be encouraged, he says, to engage in sexual behavior whenever the libidinal impulse arises in them, freely, promiscuously, and with a healthy appetite for pleasure. But Plato does not make these suggestions because he thinks that sex, or indiscriminate pleasurability, is inherently good or beautiful. On the contrary, the sexual permissiveness that he recommends is designed to harness, and eventually to eliminate, the sexual drive by causing its initial fervor to burn itself out at an early age. Growing children can then direct their affective energies toward higher interests that transmute the sexual into a passion for the ideal, for the good and beautiful as abstract essences that show forth the objective being of reality.

Many a Christian saint could find in this Platonic notion a program for cleansing the soul of its inevitable sinfulness. It would be erroneous, however, to think that Platonist or saint aspired toward anything similar to what Nietzsche called a "spiritualizing" of sex. That was a possibility, to which I return in a later chapter, that Nietzsche entertains as a defense of sexual love. He was trying to see how sex itself, as an instinctual and explicitly physical response, might be infused with spiritual meaning that would elevate it from within. Plato and his followers had no desire to accord this type of idealization to the sexual. They wanted to substitute a different attitude, a love that is not besmirched by the imperfections that adhere to everything sensory and material. When they recommended liberated behavior among the young, they did so because they were convinced that a satiety of experience would prove to the developing boy or girl that sexual pleasure is not worth the frustration, the agony, the mental pain that are unavoidable even when sexuality exists without parental and social interference. The Platonists did not believe that sex, or sexual love itself, can encompass an acceptable ideal of goodness relative to its own definition.

In Freud's reliance upon traditional thinking about sex and love, we find a further exemplification of this ambivalence. Freud is, in fact, a point of departure for its importance in the modern world. Though he occasionally tried to dignify his conception of love by claiming Plato as a precursor, Freud derived his views more immediately from Schopenhauer and other philosophic pessimists of the nineteenth century. They, too, acknowledged their indebtedness to Plato. Freud and Schopenhauer were right to do so. Like them Plato believed that empirical science, correctly understood, would substantiate the metaphysical dualism that provided a framework for knowledge about reality. But the science available to Plato was primitive and could hardly bolster nineteenth-century philosophizing. Moreover, the great post-Romantic emphasis upon affect as the all-pervading energy of organic nature—the will in Schopenhauer, libido in Freud—led them toward approaches largely inimical to Plato's faith in pure reason.

The Freudian idea of "rationalization" was explicitly designed to show how often human beings delude themselves by means of reason, rather than using it beneficially to uncover truths that nothing else can discern. For Freud, sexuality is basically nature's energy geared to the needs of reproduction. But libido of this sort is physical, not at all a craving for perfection or ideality. Love being reducible to aim-inhibited sex, it too could have none of the metaphysical meaning Plato suggested.

As Freud interprets it, idealization is necessarily illusory. It consists in "overvaluation" of its object; it is an "overestimation" that signifies how reason can be distorted by affective impulse. Freud does not deny that sexual love manifests an idealizing strain in human nature, and he recognizes that it may be true to reality in the sense that it issues from our wanting to flourish and survive in the world of material existence. But Freud also insists that this attitude usually falsifies whatever we need or desire. That happens because the idealistic view of reason lures us into inflated, even transcendental, expectations about the extrasexual consummations that love can possibly afford. In all of this, Freud's thought is totally different from Plato's.

A similar rejection of Plato had occurred in the writings of Schopenhauer. He describes the will as absolutely random and devoid of prearranged goals, whether ideal or not. From the perspective of human aspiration, the will is hideous, without meaning in itself, and evil in its effect upon all living entities, which must nevertheless serve its desire to exist. Since will is nothing but the universal effort toward self-preservation, it deploys sexual love as a circuitous mechanism for generating the human species among others. In order to function successfully, Schopenhauer argues, interpersonal love deceives both participants into thinking they are motivated by sentiments that are benevolent and largely idealistic. In reality, they are driven by an urge to continue the race through physical means that material nature has ordained. The rest is only window-dressing.

While reorienting Plato in this fashion and preparing the ideological context for Freud's scientistic efforts, Schopenhauer also charts affective regions that neither he nor Freud explores sufficiently. Apart from his metaphysics of love between the sexes, Schopenhauer presents a theory about compassion as the basis of morality. Though Plato described the good society that would enable individuals to fulfill their innate capacities in harmony with other members of the group, his longing for all-resolving Reason negates any great reliance upon feelings, even moral feelings like compassion. Idealistic notions about indiscriminate love of humanity, or even of those who suffer, Freud rejects because he thinks this love may never yield any benefit to oneself. In both Plato and Freud the appraisive element of valuation excludes any Schopenhauerian appeal for compassionate feeling toward fellow sufferers in the tragedy of life.

Schopenhauer's notion of compassion is deficient in ways that we need not go into here.[2] At the same time, I admire his repudiation, as a naturalist, of Plato's concept of idealization. Like Freud, he is in fact a cynical reviler of Platonic idealism. For Schopenhauer and Freud ideals are not the exemplars of a benign and well-ordered universe to which a priori Reason is attuned. On the contrary, they insist that ideals emerge from primal fields of force, ultimately physical, that show themselves in the material and appetitive determinants of human nature. Neither Schopenhauer nor Freud appreciated the fact that imagination is a creative faculty that modifies these determinants before they can have their effect upon us. But, if I am right, there is no other way that we can understand how sex, love, and compassion function either separately or in their common ricochet.

This blindness in Schopenhauer and in Freud dates back to Plato and persists in Western philosophy almost to the present. Though little rectification could be made at the time, various Romantic authors of the nineteenth century tried to explain one or another type of affective attachment by reference to imagination as both a source and companion of idealization. Shelley claimed that the same kind of imagination that goes into poetry is needed for anyone to be truly humane or moral. The early Schlegel, in *Lucinde* for example, argued that sex turns into sexual love through acts of imagination that are both consummatory and ethical.

A long tradition in literature had prepared the way for this modern development. In the poetry of Ovid and Catullus in the ancient world, in the northern version of medieval courtly love as exemplified by *The Romance of the Rose* and *Carmina Burana*, in the writings by empirical philosophers in later centuries, one finds hints about imagination as it infuses sexuality even when sex does not culminate as love. Nevertheless the vastly dominant approach of those who spoke about such matters suffered from the same shortcoming as in Plato, Schopenhauer, and Freud. Sexuality was traditionally assumed to be a quasi-mechanical phenomenon operating through chemical or other physiological springs whose activation occurs without the involvement of either imagination or idealization. And though the love of humanity, whether or not it takes the form of compassion, could be recognized as adherence to moral and religious ideals, it too was not considered an offshoot of imagination.

I am suggesting that all affective attachments involve imaginative processes that are definitive of them. But I can show this only by portraying imagination in its dialectical interplay with idealization, which I interpret as just the human proclivity to make ideals.

✳

In his attempt to amalgamate the best in Plato, Schopenhauer, Freud, and to some extent Henri Bergson, Marcel Proust took upon himself the needed transition from the rationalism we have been discussing to a kind of vitalism that perceives the inner tie between imagination and idealization while also emphasizing that their combined influence permeates all affective realities.

Reduced to its essentials, the Proustian perspective depicts sexuality, love, benevolent concern, and even friendship—in general, the entire gamut of positive feelings toward other persons—as a class of responses to what Proust calls an "image" that we have created in our unceasing effort to possess some object of desire. This image that we invent and then pursue originates in part from our sensory acuities. But Proust recognizes that it also embodies imagination as it modulates their effect upon us. In some of the many affective situations that he analyzes, Proust does give special importance to visual imagery. But by the time he formulates his doctrine of essences at the end of *A la recherche du temps perdu*, he invokes a much broader concept of imagination. He sees it as relevant to sensations of every sort. He even suggests, occasionally, that nonvisual images might have the deepest importance in our being.

Throughout his writing, Proust treats the image as an expression of values that often matter only to the lover. As Proust conceives of it, the image is an agency of idealization inasmuch as it projects ideals that arise from the lover's imaginative attempt to procure the maximum fulfillment of natural impulses. As a product of imagination and idealization, the image is a personal creation. Proust treats it as a typically human invention designed to possess not only the physical being of other people (or things, or ideals) but also their hidden reality. The image reflects the nature of both its object and its originator. At the same time, Proust insists that the image is a veil or quasi-mirror that hides from us whatever we are seeking so desperately to ensnare. Hence the narcissism and masochism he portrays time and again in his study of human feeling.

Hence also the conclusions about affective attachment that Proust finally reaches. They are as follows: Given our bifurcated state, divided between our craving for objective truth and our imprisonment within the cell of human subjectivity, all our striving for consummatory oneness must fail; the more intense our yearning or emotional need, the more damaging will the experience of failure be; as the most imperious embodiment of imagination coupled with idealization, sexual love—and interpersonal love as a whole—is based on wish fulfillments, or even self-deceptions, that lead to psychological disease and spiritual decay.

According to Proust, the cure for this ontological disaster is a radical withdrawal from affective attachments of almost every type. The love of art is the sole exception Proust admits, but only because we thereby escape the duplicity of idealization and imagination as they exist in ordinary life. No one but the artist, or the devotee of art, he thinks, is able to transform the falsifying allure of these two faculties into a truthful depiction of what the real world recurrently promises but never delivers.

Proust sees the transmutation of the real into the aesthetic as a spiritual feat. He uses religious language to describe it, and he believes that one cannot approximate it without creative talent of the sort that he developed in himself. One had to be a philosophical realist who sees through the seductiveness of both idealization and erroneous imagination.

In the third volume of *The Nature of Love*, I criticize Proust's philosophy as a distortion that misconstrues the means by which men and women fulfill their need for affective attachment. In claiming that only the love of art is truly satisfying, Proust neglects the art of living a good life that can exist as well in sex or interpersonal love, or in any other disposition capable of providing meaning and happiness. The idealization of art that Proust espouses may be defensible, but only if we apply the concept of art much more broadly than he did. The joyfulness of love need not be limited to the achievements of a musician or sculptor or homme de lettres.[3]

While noting this myopia in the Proustian outlook, we may still acknowledge its profound awareness about the innovative power of both idealization and imagination. Only Proust's conclusions are obnoxious. Deceptive as passionate love may sometimes be, it does not inherently promote an illusory image. Nor need it foist upon its object the attributes a lover subjectively desires. Through its bestowal of value it constructs a mini-world, an affective oneness, a unique and completely personal interweaving of imagination and idealization which constitutes this form of love. Since the outcome is a new reality resulting from that creation, neither imagination nor idealization is in itself illusional. If they can be called subjective, it is merely in the sense that they belong to the attitude of men and women who orient their individual being toward this particular unification.

For each participant in the relationship, affective attachments arise out of values that have been chosen to construct the self one will now become. In being the making of ideals, a talent human beings have supremely, idealization proffers guidelines for deciding which objects, and which properties in those objects, will be the recipients of our bestowal. When Proust remarked that men fall in love with the same kind of woman over and over again, he thought he was proving the fallibility of sexual love since it mistakenly claims to have discovered some absolute identity of the beloved in each case. But actually his depiction of one attachment after another, each magnificently analyzed, displays the presence in them of something else. The narrative histories all demonstrate how idealization and imagination are creative potentialities, rather than modes of falsification. Idealization and imagination are ways of experiencing the world afresh. They are attempts to make sense of it, to decide what matters in it. They determine what shall be accepted as meaningful and important in life, not only because of appraisive goodness to be found but also because one has learned how to bestow value upon some person, thing, or ideal.

Drawing upon the Platonistic elements in his philosophy, Proust accounts for the lover's repetitive choice of blonde or slender or motherly women as a love for some universal type or essence that reveals the lover's obsessive desire to possess what this trait symbolizes. Had he wished to do so, however, he could have stressed the variability—not the uniformity—within each type. The recipients of love are never exactly the same. They differ among themselves, sometimes very greatly, as the lover moves from person to person who matters to him or her on subsequent occasions. An approach along those lines might have expunged some of the negativism and ideational ambivalence in Proust as well as Plato. Brilliant though they were, neither could find a way out of that fly bottle.

❈

The making of ideals, so prominent in our species, may be traced to cognitivist tendencies that are not wholly separable from human affect. Our intellect operates through conceptual exploration, and, at its most successful, that involves not only linguistic communication but also the ability to use it with precision and everincreasing refinement. Great mastery of the world is latent in such mental feats. They enable us to demarcate and retain for later use a store of realities that fructify a purposive response—by others in one's group as well as by oneself. But even if our intellect operates efficiently and is clearly helpful for attaining organic satisfaction, it exists in a universe that has no fixed or preestablished boundaries. We know that, good as any accomplishment may be, it could always be better. We contemplate that possibility through sheer imagination, though the system of thought that can put it into practice also requires a developed intellect.

This combination of circumstances—a cosmos that seems to be capable of infinitely greater amelioration from our point of view, an intellect whose power may well astound us, and an imagination that can conceive of almost anything—results in our having a mind that often runs the risk of becoming *over*developed. For every benefit in life there is a cost, a price that must be paid. Having managed to secure what the organism wanted in the past, the intellect can become unsettled, twisting inward and experiencing discomfort with its achievements and their persistent limitations. Knowing that in this endless cosmos the getting of what we want is no assurance that there might not also be some undiscovered *more* that one could get as well, intellect constructs ideas of what shall count as perfections. Though self-imposed, they briefly quiet the acquisitiveness of mind by formulating concepts about "that than which nothing could be greater"—or at least, better. The ideals that blossom from these figments may be infinitely remote for one reason or another, but they conjure up perfectionist goals our restless spirit can find consummatory, if only as momentary objects of contemplation.

Idealization is the enactment of this human predilection. But it is frequently hard to control as it passes through the successive stages of individual and communal evolution. Once ideals become vehicles of identification with parental figures or some integral society the parents represent, once they serve as the touchstone of our education into acceptable humanity, once they harden into looming standards of a quasi-objective sort that demand our acquiescence, once they take up residence as motivating vectors within ourselves, we may end up sacrificing many goods presently sought by some primal impulse. We do not dare to thwart the coercive aspirations that now outrank it.

Idealization is therefore a derivative nature that may sometimes be more important for human experience than the one that many naturalist philosophers consider foundational because, they believe, it is so closely kin to what exists in other animals. But this comparison among different species is moot and uninteresting. Whatever the quality and extensiveness of the kinship, idealization remains as a generic trait in humankind insofar as virtually all people have it to some extent although in devious ways. No other creature would seem to possess the perfectionism that is characteristic of idealization in our species. It is for us an aesthetic trope, yielding beauties of possible attainment that we can behold just by imagining how something might be perfect. And if perfect, completely satisfying as a shining model of what would fulfill the meaning of that object's inherent definition.

Falling short of attaining this perfection can be, and often is, a sorrow that the rest of nature need never undergo. At the same time we have access to immeasurable happiness that comes from acting in pursuit of perfections that we care about. Responding to incoming stimuli and systematically changing our behavior in accordance with our advance toward some ideal, distant as it may be, we create a value in our life that we could not find elsewhere. The geniuses in every art or science, but also saints and heroes, are able to exploit this capability. To a lesser, yet significant, degree, the same is true of most other human beings.

Idealists from Plato on have insisted that the exhilaration of striving toward a wondrous ideal is itself a perfection in life that nature has made available to us. And imagination may indeed turn this possibility into a marvelous goal for those who feel its grandeur. But actuality goes beyond mere imagining. Though we may yearn to have a life that can be conceived as perfectly engaged in the search for perfection, we must also know—unless we are out of touch with our reality—that the world usually defeats all such longing. Between the essence and the descent falls the shadow.

We therefore learn, quite early in our maturation, to expect imperfectibility in ourselves and in others. Love consists not only in treating the beloved as if he or she or they are perfect but also in admitting the fact that none of us *can* be. We manage to accept the imperfection of those we love without deluding ourselves about the undesirability of being less than perfect. Appraisal and bestowal, both essential for love to exist, are thus conjoined. We cannot live without the making of ideals or their ability to hold aloft some image of perfection. Yet all of life teaches us that, despite the splendor in the idealizing attitude, it will not long prevail against ruthless factuality.

Even the immediate consequences of idealization are often catastrophic, as in the adventures of Don Quixote. Throughout the ages Platonists have seen the sadness in this aspect of human nature. They have less often realized how glorious it can be. Though in the *Phaedrus* Plato extols the friendship that unites two men marching side by side in their progress toward absolute goodness, he fails to recognize the joy in pursuing ideals that we and others have made for reasons of our own, and whether or not they entail some image of perfection. To have our imagination aroused so strongly is itself a realization and fulfillment of much that is deep in our humanity. Regardless of how meager our success in this venture may be or seem, we thereby carry out a project that itself makes life worth living.

These remarks about idealization have relevance to all the varieties of affective attachment. Idealization invests the entire range of sex, love, and compassion as well as the spectrum of negative responses, such as revulsion, hatred, indifference, that detach us from them. Our genes may cause in us a disposition toward libidinal objects needed for reproduction of our species, but no living object can be experienced as that alone. Even if we treat a man or a woman *like* a thing, a tool for gratifying some impulse coursing through us in conformity with pressures that are largely hormonal, we are aware that our desire is nevertheless directed toward a person and not a thing. Under the pressure of our massive drive we may occlude but not eliminate entirely the residue of all that we have garnered from past experience with people similar to this one. And if the other is for us a person, however marginally, we are already subsuming him or her within a system of ideals that may well be the same for both of us.

No rapist is motivated by unadulterated lust. He wants to subjugate his victim, to reduce her to a level of inferiority that proves she has failed to satisfy whatever values, chaotically confused as they are in his perception, that he wishes to assert. Apart from the physical injury that may eventuate, rape or any other sexual act of hostility violates another's personhood. To be a person we must have the possibility of self-autonomy, freedom to decide how to use our body and our mind; we must have a capacity for moral and spiritual growth as we define them for ourselves. All this belongs to the making of ideals that matter to some particular human being. The rapist imposes his alien idealization as a means of destroying the other's independent search for whatever values are meaningful to that person. If the effort could succeed, the abused individual might indeed become a thing and not a person. Perhaps rape so often leads to murder because the rapist intuits that what functions in him as a sexual goal can be reached only by making his prey inanimate. Having been killed, a man or woman ceases to be a person and assumes in that respect the condition of a thing.

Sexual choice in general has always been understood to be partly individual and vastly subject to dissimilar ideals of beauty. The enormous female buttocks that are so attractive to men in some African cultures are often revolting to males in Western countries. But in any one society there is also a great variability of idealization. Though statistics change from one time or location to the next, what people see as sexually beguiling in each other is normally quite diverse.

To cover our ignorance in such matters we say it's all a matter of taste, or conditioning, or resemblance to some parental appearance. These ascriptions are correct insofar as they imply that no reaction has in itself a greater claim to objective value than any other. But taste, conditioning, or parental likeness operate as they do because of corresponding ideals that have been established to give meaning to our inclinations. These ideals perpetuate themselves by appearing to be worthy standards of selection. We can hardly comprehend the variety of sexual preferences without realizing that different types of idealization, all created in our imaginative search for meaning, are always active in what seems to be spontaneous sexual appetite or impulse.

In several places I have argued against the essentialistic belief that there must be a single biological norm that can, in principle, establish the relative quality of human sexual responses and even sanction conventional attitudes that exclude unrepresentative behavior. My defense of pluralism in this area has been founded on my belief that virtually all sexual choices are equally valid in themselves, issuing as they do from ideals that people prefer individually and under differing circumstances. To avoid the bigotry and downright cruelty that recur throughout the history of sex legislation, one had only to remain faithful to the pluralistic nature of idealization.

My speculations about the concept of sexual love rely upon a similar presupposition in my thought. The fruitlessness of trying to reduce attraction and affection to some essentialistic model, whether or not it incorporates biological data, has frequently been asserted in relation to love as distinct from sexuality. Many people have thought that an innate structure governs the selection of an object considered suitable for libidinal purposes, but few have claimed that anything comparable can account for love. Like the beauty that is said to reside in the eye of the beholder, love is often thought to be volatile, sporadic, and explicable by none of the goals that organisms purposively pursue. We tend to accept as veridical those abundant reports about women who fall in love with ugly men *because* they are ugly, and with even those who are repugnant morally as well as physically.

In much of life, idealization may indicate a search for perfect beauty or consummatory goodness. But love would seem to defeat this pattern. It is considered free to range as it wills, or as some unknown and possibly wayward motivation guides it. In Greek mythology love was sometimes personified as the greatest of the gods, but more commonly as an unruly boy who could destabilize the cosmic orderliness the other gods represented. Through love, human beings could make and cherish a cluster of ideals that vary not only from society to society but also from person to person.

What remained the same, at least through lengthy periods of affective evolution in the Western world, was the idealization of love itself. Belief in the ideality of love can be traced back to the ancient Egyptians. As a concept in the history of ideas, it develops not in a linear progression but in cycles and dialectically throughout the major cultures of the West. For us, who have inherited so much from the accumulated efflorescence of this ideal, it exists as a palimpsest of received assumptions though considerably battered by countervening crosscurrents in the present. We would not have the fear of love that is so current nowadays if we were less immersed in the idealization of it that continued up to and including the twentieth century.

When I was young, sexuality (as something different from love) was not idealized in the manner or degree that occurred in the 1960s and 1970s. Formerly, young women were expected to remain chaste until they married, and they were usually considered less desirable as love-objects if they had too much experience of sex or interest in it. Everything in American life encouraged girls and boys to believe that affective relations should be governed by romantic love leading up to marriage, and marital/parental love thereafter.

Apart from reproductive necessities or the expression of spousal oneness, sexuality was considered a biological force that had to be harnessed and withheld until such time as it could serve its socially acceptable role. Any other use was vilified and strenuously discouraged. The woman whose sexual behavior did not follow the restrictive mandates was liable to be punished. But if she acted as she did for reasons of love, another group of idealizations entered and caused the plot to thicken. Whether or not love might conquer all, it was accepted as an honorific sentiment that could possibly vindicate much of what would otherwise have been condemned.

The result was that women, above all those who were young, interpreted their sexual urges as proof that they were passionately in love with the person who had elicited these powerful feelings. Their responsiveness was thus subsumed under an ideal of romantic love rather than sex, the latter having been expelled from the realm of social ideality by the authorities, secular and ecclesiastical, who decided what was right or wrong.

I am not suggesting that the amatory experience engendered in this fashion was inauthentic. It existed as an obvious and mostly involuntary demonstration of what the young women surely felt. But it also reveals how pliant the ideal of love can be. The psychological scenario for young men was complementary. It was not identical, however, since the double standard in our society accorded them a freedom of sexual behavior denied to women.

The idealization of interpersonal love has been a major theme in literature and in opera. From the latter, I choose the ending of Act 1 in Puccini's *Turandot*. Far from his homeland, Prince Calaf hears about the riddles that suitors must solve if they wish to marry the heir apparent princess of Cathay. Those who fail are put to death. Seeing her from afar, Calaf can understand why she is said to be beautiful; but he has no illusions about her arrogance, her cruelty, and her pathological hatred of men. Though her father is the emperor and her spouse will inherit the throne, the prince falls in love with her as she is in herself alone.

Calaf accounts for his emotional afflatus by saying he must pursue his "glory," as he puts it. In a state of uncontrollable passion, he is beside himself when he strikes the great gong that signals his decision to vie for Turandot's hand. He is ready to lose his head literally if he cannot solve the riddles that she poses. After he does solve them, he manifests the purity of his love by releasing Turandot from her oath of marriage. He even offers to let her execute him if she learns his name. When she cannot, he freely tells her what it is. In response to this act of faith, her feelings change entirely. She falls in love with Calaf and informs the assembled court that his name is Amore (Love). He is now, for her, the embodiment of the god that personifies idealized love.

What exactly, we may ask, has Calaf experienced in his frenzy at the end of the first act? And how can it explain his subsequent behavior? What is the nature of his love? Could someone in real life fall for a creature as hideous as Turandot seems to be, and indeed is, at the beginning of the opera? I interpret the plot, which Puccini's libretto drew from a play by Gozzi in the eighteenth century, as a fable about romantic love that begins as idealization of love itself and then progresses into acceptance of another person despite her vast imperfections. From the outset Calaf reacts to the possibility of love for this unknown but challenging princess as a heroic enterprise that any adventuresome youth might find irresistible.

Being a pure-hearted nobleman, Calaf is willing to risk his life in pursuit of his idealized goal. So great is his dedication that it finally transforms the murderous Turandot into a woman who can overcome her fear of love and respond to

Calaf's authentic experience of it. When that happens, she too becomes a devotee of the idealization that has united them.

❄

Despite its slightly realistic veneer, *Turandot* is a fanciful tale, entirely suitable for the operatic stage where singing actors go beyond ordinary life as a way of expressing its affective mythology through sonic and visual devices. Though frequently embellished in this way, the idealization of love has often been presented in literature as a natural occurrence that demands the quasi-scientific verisimilitude of realistic fiction. That approach appears in Chekhov's short story "The Kiss," which scrutinizes romantic idealization with matchless honesty and wisdom.

Chekhov relates what happens to an ungainly and unerotic army officer named Ryabovich. When his unit passes through a village while on maneuvers, he is invited to an evening celebration at the home of the family of a retired general. In the company of his fellow officers, Ryabovich enjoys the food and drink but soon realizes that the hospitality being offered is mainly a formal gesture. While the others dance and make the most of this opportunity to meet handsome and appealing women, Ryabovich stays aloof. He is self-conscious about his undistinguished physical features and lack of social ease. He feels quite inept as far as casual flirtation is concerned. He has never been in love or had much sexual experience, and although he hungers for someone who might respond to his aimless ardor and whom he could marry, he hardly expects that he will ever have that joy in life.

In the course of the evening something happens accidentally that changes his existence. Having left the group, Ryabovich gets lost as he wanders through the general's large house. When he walks into a darkened room, he is surprised by footsteps and a breathless voice that whispers "At last!" At the same time "two soft, fragrant, unmistakably feminine arms were clasped about his neck; a warm cheek was pressed against his; and simultaneously there was the sound of a kiss. But at once the bestower of the kiss uttered a faint shriek and sprang away from him, as it seemed to Ryabovich, with disgust."[4]

Returning to the party, Ryabovich cannot identify the woman. Nor are there any overt consequences of his having been mistakenly kissed by her. In the detached and minutely realistic style that he employs throughout the story, Chekhov narrates the pedestrian details of Ryabovich's daily routine as an officer carrying out his normal duties during the following days and weeks. To all appearances, his life is as it always has been, unchanged by his brief encounter in the dark. But in his imagination, in his mental state, in his feelings about himself, momentous alterations have taken place. He formulates a vague but obsessive image of what the young lady must look like; he interprets the meeting she had expected as part of "an ordinary thing," a process of falling in love that comes to even unexceptional people; and he begins to feel that he himself can hope to experience something similar sooner or later.

For a while Ryabovich lives with this hope. He vaguely thinks and occasionally behaves as if he is already in love. Performing his usual ablutions in the morning, "he recalled that there was something warm and delightful in his life." Listening to the other officers recount their sexual exploits, his face has the expression of a soldier who hears "the description of a battle in which he has taken part." When his unit returns to the general's village, he is "dreamy and excited all the way, as if he was going home."[5] Ryabovich feels sure that he will see again the woman who kissed him. The idea is troublesome: "He was tortured by the question: How would he meet her? What would he talk to her about? Had she forgotten about the kiss? If the worst came to the worst, he thought, even if he did not meet her, it would be a pleasure to him merely to go through the dark room and recall the past."[6]

When he and the others reach the town, however, an invitation is not immediately forthcoming. By the time it does arrive, Ryabovich loses heart and finally sees the incident of the kiss as a haphazard event of little real significance in his life. He senses that his loveless existence will not improve. He despairs of the feelings that have buoyed him up: "And the whole world, the whole of life, seemed to Ryabovich an unintelligible, aimless jest. . . . He remembered again how Fate in the person of an unknown woman had by chance caressed him, he recalled his summer dreams and fancies, and his life struck him as extraordinarily meager, poverty-stricken, and drab."[7]

Chekhov's story is engaging, and beautifully wrought, as an illustration of what James Joyce would call narrative "epiphany"—a momentary showing forth of reality. In fact there are two epiphanies that contribute to the formal structure in this story. The terminal one, toward which the realistic writing has been pointing us from the beginning, portrays the painfulness of recognizing that life does not organize itself in accordance with our dreams and errant hopes. This is a fertile theme in Chekhov; he returns to it with great versatility in many plays and short stories. But we can reach this epiphany only after the one that arises in Ryabovich's first reaction to the kiss. It demonstrates another facet of his reality.

There are other ways in which Ryabovich might have taken what befell him in that darkened room. He could have enjoyed it as a simple pleasure—the soft and fragrant arms, the warm cheek, the charm of being kissed with ardent breathlessness.

Knowing that this preliminary consummation was not intended for him, he could have relished the serendipity of its being given by mistake, in hedonic isolation and regardless of the fact that he was not its rightful beneficiary. Had he been a sensualist, or a connoisseur in such things, he might have welcomed the event as a delicious escapade his memory could savor in the future. Or if he really thought, as some nineteenth-century Romantics did, that love is caused by fate and miraculous happenstance, he might have tried to learn the identity of this woman, not out of simple curiosity but because he felt that somehow he and she were meant for each other.

Since Ryabovich in Chekhov's tale is not that kind of person, the first, and generative, epiphany has a different configuration. It illuminates the possibility of sexual love as an attachment that begins in vivid emotion or sensuous excitation, progresses through amorphous dreams and aspirations, and then culminates in the expectation of a calm but radiant paradise of bourgeois marriage. This is the ideal that Ryabovich chooses to pursue. For a while he lives through its earlier stages. He experiences the kiss as an idealized epiphany of what may be available even to himself. Reacting to the mere embrace, he is captivated by an image of romantic love that can enrich the life of almost anyone and consequently his as well. He had previously thought he was excluded because of inadequacies in himself. Now they ceased to matter.

Without this first epiphany, the second one would have no effect, indeed could not exist. The desperation that Ryabovich finally feels, and that Chekhov understands so well, comes from his all-too-human awareness that our disabilities can make it impossible for us to attain the very ideals that we ourselves create without knowing how difficult it is to satisfy them. In this story Chekhov delineates the nature of idealization as it permeates affective imagination. He restricts himself to the romantic ideal that Ryabovich cares about, but in his presentation he shows how the interweaving of idealization and imagination imbues a sensibility whose buoyancy, followed by disenchantment, may have a devastating impact upon a person's life.

Chekhov's story investigates not only love as imaginative idealization, but also the eagerness to undergo the suffering it may bring. Not all people, possibly not Chekhov himself, might yearn so much for the routine middle-class marriage that Ryabovich idealizes. Yet many who seek some other cherished culmination could well agree that a euphoric sense of importance elevates whatever feeling or behavior that accompanies their heart's desire. This ingredient in idealization has embellished the imagination of millions throughout the history of humankind.

Even in our day, when vast segments of the population are now averse to most ideals that mattered in the past, the idealization of romantic love holds sway over many men and women. The wayward spouse will justify his or her tendency to dally sexually not by citing an appetite for pleasure or titillation but rather by claiming to have fallen in love. Though the ascription may be accurate and the emotional involvement unmistakable, that mode of explanation assumes an ideality and final validation in one's having submitted to this affective condition instead of rejecting it.

But the condition can always be resisted. Unless there is a concomitant pathology, which may need to be treated independently, love can be radically controlled and even uprooted by a person who is determined to repel what it demands. Society regularly fosters, explicitly inculcates, ethical and religious means of subduing amatory obsession, if only out of concern about the misery that others might undergo in its wake. But when romantic love becomes the ruling idealization, these considerations are relegated to a secondary status. They are not allowed to affect the lover's feelings or decisions. Emotions are often volatile, and if someone believes that romantic love condones his or her response, that alone can cause the falling in love, which is usually a plunging into it, to occur with urgency and extreme intensity.

Idealization appears in all varieties of love and in relation to every type of object toward which love is directed. In each case there is an affective substratum that can be called "natural" rather than artificial. The idealization of parental or filial love is predicated upon biological realities that are foundational in our species, as in others. Sexual, social, or religious love also emanate from organic sources that are deeply engrained. Among these natural motives, the idealization of sexual love differs from all the others in one important respect. Particularly in Western culture, it has been conveyed through a succession of impressive and extremely persuasive works of art in every medium.

One might reply that religious art has had a similar influence, and that even the idealized love of our clan or nation has been communicated through the personal heroism emblazoned in civic and military artworks. Nevertheless, the idealization of sexual love in literature, opera, and film has drawn more exhaustively upon creative imagination than has the idealizing of nonsexual love. That is certainly true today. To some degree it has been the case as long as our current media have existed.

In the *Inferno* Dante encapsulated this fact in Francesca's line: "Galeotto fu quel libro e chi lo scrisse." (That book was a Galeotto, and he who wrote it.) She is talking about the occasion on which she and Paolo yielded to carnal impulse that led to the adulterous acts for which they are now being punished. The two had been reading together a book that narrates how Galeotto (Galehot) was the intermediary between Lancelot and Queen Guinevere, and so an instrumentality in their illicit love. This story enflamed the sexual feelings of Paolo and Francesca by presenting a glamorized account of the royal personages engaging in romantic love to which they gave priority over marital and religious ties. Francesca blames the book for having been a pander that misled Paolo and herself. She condemns not only the book but also the author of it. After Francesca finishes her woeful tale, Dante faints—as if to acknowledge that authors like himself who write romantic literature must take responsibility for harmful idealizations that they embroider and even create anew by means of their literary talent.

We may wonder why the art forms I mentioned— literature, opera, film—should be so greatly given over to the idealization of sexual love. And why have they not equally promulgated social and religious love? In the case of film, a plausible answer comes quickly to mind. That art dates from a time when Romantic philosophies had been spreading their message across the Western world and beyond. As romanticism affirmed the holy goodness of interpersonal intimacy, films devoted themselves to the showing forth of what many people in our era have valued most in their affective life: namely, the attainment of consummatory sex. The cinematic imagination could express that part of our being with a graphic vibrancy that no other art form can emulate.

But also film employed, and was permitted to exploit, voyeuristic techniques that magnified the idealization of sexuality in ways that were forbidden to rival arts. The showing of physical intercourse or total nudity or sexual violence realistically portrayed was taboo in early films, but their simulacra could be flashed on the screen as vivid presentations of the search for sexual completion in conformance with the idealizations of romanticism. In establishing its distance between the spectators and the images they saw, the technology of cinema imposed a minimal respectability despite the prurience of what was being displayed.

A similar development had occurred, many centuries before, in the history of fictional literature. Literary arts, whether in poetry or prose, have a mesmerizing effect only for those who enjoy a kind of imagination that is no less specialized than in film. Readers must learn how to translate the narrator's words into possibilities they derive from the printed page. Moreover, when the text includes descriptions or conceptual elaborations, they must delve into the imaginary component of their imagination without the aid of visual cues that pictorial or photographic images provide. This necessity imposes its own kind of distance. It can be readily diminished, but that requires a learning process, which occurs in literature less immediately than in film or a staged musical production.

With their power to overwhelm the senses while also retaining semblances of real men and women seen or heard, film and opera have an exceptional ability to imprint upon their somewhat passive recipients any image of affective humanity they wish to convey. This gives these art forms an advantage over literature. At the same time, literature has had much success as a proselytizing medium. Like the other two, it has been an efficient Galeotto for the arousal and revision of ideals that continually promulgate whatever we value in our affective attachments. Therein consists the growth of civilization.

But even to talk about "civilization" implies ideals that are often different from the sexual or interpersonal. People who say they want to leave this world a better place than when they arrived are expressing an allegiance to social, possibly religious, goals that cannot be reduced to the ideality either of sex or of love for some other person. Whatever idea they may have about that better world, those who want to bring it into being are attaching their humanitarian feelings to a distant but morally honorific end they find especially significant. Since they have in mind the general condition of the world, and since they are thinking about a time when they will not be alive, their affective disposition bespeaks a projective love whose culmination is not likely to benefit them in any way.

One might say that philanthropists are rewarded by the happiness they have in thinking that their concern is rendered meaningful by the goodness for others that they will someday have created. Even so, this possible goodness must be experienced by unborn generations, whose putative and as yet nonexistent welfare matters to those of us who make the appropriate idealization in the present. Our own personal interest is not its motivating principle.

I am intrigued by the ideal of leaving the world a better place because its open texture makes it so unclear. The idealization becomes more focused, and more problematic, once we ask ourselves how we can justify our introducing into that new world what we consider improvements. For all we know, the future human beings may not be grateful for our intervention. Are we right in assuming that what we call "better" will even interest them? Are we possibly manipulating their reality, imposing upon them a fait accompli that they must cope with as best they can? Parents have often behaved that way with their children. But if our benevolence consists in changing the world to suit our own conception of a good life whether or not the eventual inhabitants agree with us about it, wherein lies the ideality of our intention? It would seem to be a form of aggressive arrogance rather than a genuine love for what is good from the beneficiaries' unknowable point of view.

Groucho Marx is reported to have said: "Why do anything for posterity? What has posterity done for you?" We laugh because the bold and delicious cynicism of this imaginative quip jolts us in our acquiescence to an idealization that few people question. But it may also be taken seriously. Freud would seem to have done so, since he repudiated the ideal of turning the other cheek, or feeling love for one's enemies, or loving human beings simply because they are human.

Freud believed that nonappraisive love is either disingenuous or insidious because, he thought, it usually amounts to self-love on our part and may in fact be injurious both to ourselves and to those we claim to care about. Though his conception of bestowal was very sketchy—his criticism of it is implied but undeveloped—Freud finds humanitarian attitudes always suspect and often hazardous. He may be right. The creation of values without which life would have no meaning is always dangerous, particularly when it involves persons with whom we have no immediate or proximate connection. Neither Freud nor anyone else can avoid this predicament.

The perils in bestowal that Freud warns us about vary with the different forms of social and religious attachment. He himself was distressed by the sorrow and the harm that romantic love can wreak; he saw it as overvaluation that tends to cause depletion of the lover's ego. But he recognized the value of friendship, and even loving-kindness toward the children of one's friends. He accepts such attachments because they belong to the network of purposive bonds that are needed for an individual to survive. People cannot be friends unless they try to help one another. This benefits each of them and tends to include those who receive their individual love, above all their children. Freud was convinced that whatever bestowals go beyond these appraisive boundaries can only be foolishness or a stumbling block, as Saint Paul said about Romans or Jews who rejected the selflessness of Christian love. Like those earlier critics, Freud saw no virtue in the idealization of indiscriminate love. He denied that it reveals the nature of either social or religious worth.

In taking this position, Freud neglects the deeply rooted ideals that lie at the opposite pole from the libidinal energy he posits as basic in human instinct. Though recognizing the important role of identification with parents or secular and ecclesiastic leaders who then become "ego ideals," Freud misconstrues not only sympathy and empathy but also compassion. Such modes of idealization are more erratic and unstable than the ones he denotes as fundamental in group development. And yet, the feelings he repudiates can sometimes have a far greater impact than the self-oriented dispositions he adduces.[8]

For one thing, sympathy and compassion, or even empathy, presuppose and often evoke a pool of imagination that may well become a flood. This will not occur on all occasions. In his book on morals and legislation Jeremy Bentham remarks with horror that many people casually walk by a drunk lying in the gutter and never bother to turn the man's head or otherwise make sure that he does not drown in his own vomit. The people Bentham mentions were doubtless well-meaning persons. But they lacked that imaginative acuity that Shelley celebrates as a precondition for true morality. Had they allowed idealizations needed for sympathy or compassion to activate the requisite response, their imagination would have awakened in them an awareness of the hurt that the unattended drunk might suffer as well as the ease with which they could prevent it.

Shelley's allusion to what he calls "sympathetic identification" occurs in his defense of poetry and the humanities as a whole. He claims that these pursuits are outstanding in their ability to communicate the quality of human life wherever it occurs. They can help us to put ourselves in another's position, to understand the world from his or her experiential point of view, and therefore to imagine what that person craves or detests, finds agreeable or vile, good or evil. This idea is very persuasive, and especially timely nowadays when the humanities in most technological societies are more threatened than ever before. But Shelley's overall conception is incomplete. Aside from difficulties that stem from his amalgamation of sympathy and compassion, which are not the same, his analysis falls short in two essential ways.

The first of these turns upon the origin of the idealizing imagination that Shelley commends. He correctly associates it with an appreciative attitude toward life itself which the art of poetry preeminently cultivates. Though Shelley does not say as much, this affirmative attitude is latent, but usually hidden, in virtually all human beings. Shelley insists that "A man, to be greatly good, must imagine *intensely* and *comprehensively*."[9] I have italicized these words in order to highlight their reference to an extraordinary degree of achievement. Yet imagination can hardly reach such august heights by itself and on most occasions. It needs to be pruned, refined and educated, propelled to a level at which it can elicit powers that may be there in everybody but put to use in relatively few of us.

Shelley's defense of the humanistic arts would have been more impressive if he had shown that they are attuned, however obliquely, to moral education that most people do not have but may sorely need. Visionary that he is, Shelley contemplates a possibility of perfect morality without attending to its evolution out of the imperfect welter of ordinary life. The relevant idealizations are often endangered there, inchoate and always requiring further development.

The second deficiency in Shelley's fervent (and inspiring) statement comes from his not facing up to something Schopenhauer would have emphasized almost automatically. That is the role that suffering plays in the creation of morality. Compassion comes into existence as a human ideal because we identify with those who are fellow creatures in a cosmic order that has no interest in the permanent welfare of any of its participants. Rousseau was mistaken in treating compassion as if it were the same as pity, but he might have been right when he said that neither would occur if people did not fear that they too could someday experience whatever evils had befallen those toward whom they extend their humanitarian feelings. Would we even notice the mental and physical pain that others feel unless we had had similar misfortune in ourselves? There is much of life that we can understand only through suffering, though that is what we least desire. Our ability to have the type of interpersonal imagination that is essential for compassion to become a viable ideal might never amount to very much if we were immune from the agonies that pervade all the rest of life.

Plato wondered how the gods could be thought to love anything, since they have a being that is perfectly good and lacks nothing that is desirable. As a corollary to his reflection, he might also have reasoned that compassionate love is a significant possibility for human beings because our deprivations and recurrent misery cause us to identify with those who are similar in this respect, or even more unhappy.

That is the wisdom and pathetic capability that King Lear finally acquires in Shakespeare's play.

Even so, Hume did well to go beyond Rousseau. Hume rightly insisted that humanitarian inclinations, however meager they may be, are native to our being and not just derivative from selfish concern or anxiety about our own vulnerability. While focusing upon the actual or potential distress of a fellow creature, compassion extends a kindly, friendly, and companionate feeling toward the person or animal we wish to help. Compassion is a type of love, and it easily coalesces with the love that can belong to friendship.

As an ideal of humane behavior, compassion is evident in the attitude of a doctor or therapist who shows love for his or her patients by responding in a thoroughly professional way to whatever problems they may have. It appears in the devotion to their pets that animal lovers feel, but also in their tolerance for the lower intellect of this chosen dog or cat, and for its lack of any moral sense that human beings recognize. The same applies to paternal forbearance toward a child whose maturation at an age of innocence permits it to enjoy pampered freedoms, and even selfishness, that adults are not allowed. Much of what we consider saintliness is not only the doing of good things for others but, additionally, the fact that they are done as an overt affirmation of compassionate oneness that manifests acceptance and good will.

❈

As I have suggested, Plato's pregnant error consisted in defining true love as love for the highest form, the Good or Beautiful, and then insisting that only pure Reason can lead us to this attachment. But Plato was entranced by his notion of a culminating essence because he saw it as universal, abstract, and eternally irradiating whatever we or other creatures are able to experience in the temporality of our lives. The metaphor of the sun that Plato uses at several junctures is wholly appropriate to his philosophy. In its infinite bounty the Platonic Good or Beautiful bestows itself unstintingly upon all earthly existence. That is why the Christians were able to reinterpret it as an attribute of God, whose agapastic love descends upon everything.

Neither Plato nor the Christians could believe that human nature is rich enough to encompass within itself the feelings of empathy, sympathy, and compassion that can reach out indefinitely toward other persons. Plato acknowledged no such indiscriminate love. The Christians thought that only a divinity like the one they imagined could effect so marvelous an achievement. Both Plato and the Christians refused to countenance the possibility that nature alone, finite and fallible as it is in us, could ever engender anything of the sort.

I am not saying that this part of our affective nature can exist without being accompanied by selfish and appraisive inclinations. My view of idealization is not idealistic. I am prepared to think that selfishness is always present in us. And while I do not agree with Freud's belief that sexual libido reveals the ultimate character of love in general, I can see the merit in his saying that the libidinal is often unbridled in its object-choice, and therefore prone to express itself through behavior that is not itself sexual. In opposition to what Freud or Plato or the Christians maintain, however, I find no justification for trying to reduce ideals of compassion or humanitarian love into affective responses vastly different from them.

Since compassion is necessary for romantic as well as social and religious love, as I think, it overlaps with them. It has a distinctive place in the range of human affect, and is recognizable by those who want to transcend our material limitations as well as by those who feel we should accept them as they are. In either event, compassion serves as a separate and definitive ideal, not derivative from any other.

Like all ideals, compassion waxes and wanes in group as well as individual history. The boy or girl who thoughtlessly destroys, and even tortures, a lower form of life might find alternate amusements if he or she grew up in a Hindu community where ants beneath the table are sometimes offered bits of food. This is done as an act of communal oneness toward creatures that suffer as we do in karma's merciless cycle. By promoting this identification with them, society can encourage a joyful sense of kinship, and deeply felt commiseration. The compassionate attachment exists equally in both sentiments. In primitive life the former was enacted in rituals we no longer practice nowadays. But in our recent wariness about the ecological calamities that beset all life on earth, we makers of the modern world may at least be fostering a more wholesome sensitivity to the tragedies that other species increasingly endure.

This larger consciousness mainly eventuates in behavior that is prudential for ourselves, protective of our own race. But also it can lead us to take upon our shoulders the hardships faced by every inhabitant of this planet. To do that is to move in the direction of a love of life. For some this can even be a love for the love that any living entity may experience, if only in loving itself. Spiritual affects of this type exist in persons who have the idealizing imagination that compassion germinates more or less indiscriminately. And finally, we might remark that insofar as compassion is needed for sex and romantic love to reach fruition as modes of attachment, it brings them too within the orbit of religious or quasi-religious idealization.

Few of the traditional religions have chosen to idealize in this fashion. Even those that sought to embrace a love of

nature have usually transfigured it through theological
doctrines that subordinate the compassion in human beings
to some greater glory of divinity. The religious attitude that
I am proposing is scorned by most religions that have
managed to endure thus far. It avoids all dogmas that foster
ideals inimical to both the love of life and the love of love in
life. My conception is dedicated single-mindedly to the
belief that sex, love, and compassion are internally related.
On my view these three are interwoven, merely but
gloriously, as products of spirit emerging in the world
through affective attachments available to our species and
consummatory in themselves.

3

Consummation

Imagination and idealization are autotelic: their end or purpose lies within themselves; they are governed by inner rules that can attain a momentum of their own. In the throes of some powerful inspiration, an artist may become oblivious of anything that might impede the pursuit of his imaginative ideals. Even the absent-minded professor may be mentally absent from commonplace realities because his or her imagination keeps steering itself toward ideal possibilities considered more important. But in itself this does not explain the affective tug that binds us to some thing or person or valued goal. Either directly or indirectly, there must be a payoff that warrants the energy invested in imagination, in idealization, and in their continual interaction.

That essential recompense is consummatory gratification serving as a mainstay of affective experience. I choose this terminology, and the concepts that go with it, for two reasons. First, the word *consummation* is broad enough in its intentional scope to cover the entire range of human feeling. At one extreme, its relevance to sexual responsiveness is obvious, since that often involves organic processes, physiological urgencies, ordinarily impelled toward some completion. When these processes reach that culmination, it is as if their native fuel has been totally consumed, burned off, transformed into a cool and welcome afterglow of satisfaction. Yet consummation can also signify a fulfillment of interests that are actively nourished as incipient values, and hence as spiritual opportunities that go beyond what is solely material. This portion of the spectrum includes love in all its varieties. But what about the region in which fellow feeling, friendship, empathy, sympathy, and compassion exist? They would seem to be more obscure than sex or interpersonal love. How and of what, we may ask, can they be consummatory?

One might reply that human beings are *programmed* to want social, as well as personal, attachment to other living entities. This kind of bond can occur through identifications effected by ties like sympathy and compassion. Though some such notion may be valid, it seems strange that we should be innately motivated to seek out the miseries of others and to take them upon ourselves in the emphatic manner of compassionate involvement. Being an ethical and religious response, compassion must find its rewards through consummations that are neither clearly evident nor invariable. These derive from our need to believe that we are part of a universe in which beneficent feelings make a difference.

Though the cosmos would appear to be unconcerned about anything its individual creatures value, we bestow a caring attitude just by reacting affirmatively to other animate beings, and by manifesting our oneness with them *because* they either suffer or are liable to do so. Rootless and afraid as people may be in a world without meaning, they find a haven for themselves by identifying with persons or forms of life in a similar plight. They therein achieve a consummation of vital and unifying impulsions that are embedded in our nature.

The second reason I choose the term *consummation* is more technical, more closely related to the history of ideas about human affect. In their attempt to characterize the impetus behind or beneath our appetitive behavior, philosophers and psychologists use language that is sometimes hedonistic, sometimes mechanistic, and frequently reductivistic. Since affective attachments were thought to arise from organic needs, it seemed appropriate to link our feelings and our cravings to a quest for sensory gratifications. These are usually discrete and quantifiable in one manner or another, and consequently amenable to scientific investigation. But the values in life are more complex than this would indicate. They are rarely explicable by reference to positive charges localized in a single moment of sensorial excitation. Though a sense experience can be highly satisfying in itself and correctly described as a pleasure, enjoyment, or hedonic delight, the extensiveness of its potentialities results from the wider and more comprehensive states implied by the notion of consummatory fulfillment.

In deference to its generality, we may possibly think of consummation as the "final" goal of animate existence. Not final in the sense of being terminal or without further moments in time. Nor yet as that which justifies whatever conduct succeeds in being consummatory. But rather as the beckoning outcome that all living things seek as a harmonious quiescence of their inner pulsations. If we respond sympathetically to this aspiration in others, we experience a derivative, but distinct, consummation within ourselves.

To recognize the importance of this attitude, we need only touch upon traditional doctrines about religious love. Odd as it may be, the assertion that God *is* love articulates a faith in the consummational goodness of everything "he" has created, which is to say, everything that exists. This does not mean that each existent being is good rather than bad or evil. And neither does it mean that the good ones attain their goodness through a consummation of their personal or accidental wants. On the contrary, we are told that those who have "good religion" will restrain and even eradicate many of their desires in order to conform to God's predestined plan.

Where then does the relevant consummation reside? Presumably in the all-embracing structure of God's arrangements, in the ontological totality of being that God has chosen for this world. Members of the human race being free to accept or reject the intentions of divinity, they may seek other consummations on their own. But since these belong willy-nilly to existence as a whole, they too show forth the efficacy of God's creative bestowal, even when they militate against it. So pervasive is God's love assumed to be that it engulfs any hateful (but unavailing) evil that tries to contravene it.

This kind of belief is always fraught with logical problems. I will not delineate them here. People who are willing to swallow such difficulties often do so for the sake of the all-resolving optimism in the theological conception. Having a need to feel that reality is consummatory in its totality—that nothing is completely frustrated or irremediably lost in the overall scheme of creation—large segments of our species will always cling to whatever dogma conduces to that sentiment. Moreover, the cosmic consummation portrayed by a comforting escatology is normally presented in terms that are metaphoric of other consummations that have more immediate relevance to everyday life.

This is apparent throughout the affective attachments that matter in the moment-by-moment existence of most men and women. Freud was not needed for reflective people to realize that the Father which is in heaven and the Mother of the Son who offers universal redemption are themselves the consummation of what we all hope for in an idealized father, mother, or older brother. By accepting these imaginative idealizations we are able to have, at once and concretely, satisfying feelings akin to the ethereal consummations depicted in religious imagery. We know that God the Father is not a father like our own; we surmise, and for many this becomes an article of faith, that the nature of the deity cannot be conveyed by any image; and yet we can find sustenance in believing that the supremacy of this benign creator consists in his ability to actualize our conception of perfected paternity.

The sustenance to which I refer includes a consummatory attitude toward the universe in its entirety. Instead of cringing because it is a hostile or indifferent chaos of violent forces beyond our comprehension, which one may well believe, we experience the world as a place where we can feel more or less at home. The feeling of at-home-ness has enormous resonance for us. The consummations incorporated in it reverberate throughout human feeling at its most satisfying.

Unless they are pantheists, those who have the faith I have been describing deny that the meaning of God, or of the other personages in the theological mythology, can be reduced to sought-for consummations in the temporal, mainly material world. I do not disagree. Without sharing this worldview, I believe that neither imagination nor idealization operates in the crude fashion that some naturalists take for granted. I have no reason to deny that belief in the inherent goodness of the cosmos may engender consummatory sentiments not at all the same as any pertaining to limited fulfillments in nature. Though often very meaningful, most consummatory occurrences are specific and their origins usually traceable—though not reducible—to prior experience. We can remember, for instance, the times we felt at home with parents who seemed capable of protecting and preserving us. The cosmic consummations are different because they are predicated upon ideas of totality, infinity, eternity, and even a mode of being outside time and space. Nevertheless the two types overlap. We could not make sense of the latter without the former, and there is nothing in the particularity of the former to exclude the latter.

This amorphous state of affairs is characteristic not only of imagination and idealization but also of consummation as it exists in our species. When anything satisfies, wholly or even partly, we feel that all's right with the universe. And in a sense, it is. Having eaten a good meal, we could not have our pleasant feeling of repleteness unless the stars in their constellations were harmoniously poised as a causal setting for our momentary enjoyment. A cosmic explosion, which could happen at any time, would have canceled in advance any agreeable occasion that comes to us. In this regard, all of life is a serendipity, even when it is overladen with evils we must avoid. Our panoramic view of the universe, as created either by a loving progenitor or by mindless energy conforming to laws of physics, cannot be the same as our beliefs about the prosaic gratifications that issue from organic drives. But neither are these ideational clusters completely unrelated to each other.

When Christ in the gospels explains the mystery of his death by saying "it is consummated," he means that God's benevolent design has now revealed itself. Baffling as it may be, that is a soothing notion. We respond accordingly because it reassures us about the death we all face. Life has no sting if it, as well as the ending of it, provides consummations such as this one. If our days are geared to a rhythmic harmony of what the psychologists call appetitive and consummatory behavior, we may experience both happiness and a sense of ultimate meaning in relation to that reality. The appetitive needs activate our purposive explorations, and the consummatory termination of each pursuit rewards us in the present while also renewing our ability to continue the trajectory of good life. The message that the Christian myth announces seeks to transcend, and give a joyful clarification of, these empirical facts. The myth proclaims that even death, which destroys the natural continuum of ends and means, is consummatory and not the calamity that it might otherwise seem to be. It is a completion that brings life to its appointed destination. Those who have grace are thus sustained in their confidence that they will attain a perfect consummation in being attached to God forevermore.

In Hamlet's speech about suicide, Shakespeare plays imaginatively with these ideas. Death is said to be "a consummation devoutly to be wished," which any Christian might affirm. But then the "dread of something after death" counters this expression of religious faith. The unknowability of what lies beyond not only puzzles the will to suicide but also inhibits the orthodox belief about a desired eventuality we may hopefully anticipate. When, in the final act, Hamlet remarks that "the readiness is all," he enunciates still another attitude toward death. To be ready for death is to accept it as a natural quietus for what has gone before. As the character in *Cymbeline* suggests, death may be perceived as a "quiet consummation." So too does a fruit silently reach the preestablished ripeness that makes it ready to be gathered.

In his *Ode to a Nightingale* Keats reports that being happy in the bird's expression of its own happiness, he feels that "Now more than ever seems it rich to die, / To cease upon the midnight with no pain, / While thou art pouring forth thy soul abroad / In such an ecstasy!" This idea of death as an apogee of total consummation in the experience that precedes it also appears when Otello declares, at the beginning of Verdi's opera, that his love for Desdemona is so great he wishes to die at that very moment.

In a less histrionic manner, we can agree that death may curtail but not negate the goodness of a life that has reached its proper consummation in having fully used the potential forces that comprised its place in nature. No reference to a different realm of being is needed.

❄

I am told that the poet Tennyson wept at the realization that in a hundred years or so none of his contemporaries would still be alive. He obviously saw no possibility of consummation in their death. But does the succession of generations, one after another, merit unremitting despair? Instead of shedding tears, can we not say to all those who have died, and to those who will, and projectively to ourselves: "home art gone and ta'en thy wages"? Particularly if one thinks—as Hegel did—that in the passage of time humanity moves forward to the fulfillment of higher ideals, can one not believe that each death may contribute to some as yet unrealized consummation?

I am not convinced that such replies truly understand the quality of Tennyson's feeling. He was responding to the fact that even the most talented or sensitive or beautiful people we might meet in life will be annihilated within a matter of decades, at most. For all of them as individuals, and for all of us in general, our approaching dissolution is not consummatory but immeasurably destructive. On this view, death is the enemy of the human spirit, and though our existence can sometimes be amply gratifying while it continues, its ending would scarcely seem to be a consummation. We may possibly reconcile ourselves to the frailty of our material being. That is just a manifestation of the universal recycling process that operates throughout the cosmos. But the abolition of all the thoughts, feelings, hopes, dreams, imaginative aspirations—the fine and noble ones nullified as well as those that are crass and ugly—may well seem horrifying to us. How can this fatality be considered good under any circumstances? The sheer finitude of life might strike us as precluding any final consummation.

In the Western world the myth that best represents man's discovery that he is irredeemably subject to the limitations of mortality, and therefore capable of enjoying only sporadic consummations, occurs in *Genesis*. After Adam and Eve have transgressed by eating the fruit of the tree of the knowledge of good and evil, they are driven out of Eden lest they partake of the tree of life and so exist eternally. We are not told why God wants to deny everlasting life to human beings, as we also remain ignorant of why they should have no knowledge of good and evil. God only remarks (disparagingly) that since man has eaten the forbidden fruit he has "become as one of us." The hapless couple are therefore chastised and fettered in their being.

The serpent had spoken the truth when he said that Eve would not die, as God had predicted, on the very day that she or Adam ate the fruit of this one tree. They die subsequently, after they have been cast into the hardship of life outside Eden. But when they transgressed, neither of

them even knew what the tree of life signified, and they had
no awareness of what mortality might or might not entail.
Having discovered the meaning of good and evil, their first
experience is to feel ashamed of being naked. But how can
there be anything shameful about that? Is this shamefulness
part of our knowledge about good and evil, or does it
pertain to something else? And if Adam and Eve are now "as
one of us," does this indicate that a similar sentiment is felt
by all the angels and by God himself?

I mention these inscrutable questions in order to break
free from the received interpretation of the myth. As often
happens in stories of this type, cause and effect have been
subtly interchanged. What the fable actually teaches human
beings is that the governing forces in the universe will not
permit them to live as long or as pleasantly as they would
like, and that knowledge of good and evil reveals what they
stand to lose. Not only does such knowledge result from
guilt they have somehow brought upon themselves, but also
it causes them to be uniquely distressed about their natural
state of being. They are animated by a spirit that renders
them unlike the other animals, who are ignorant of good
and evil and so incapable of feeling guilt or shame. On the
other hand, men and women cannot expect to emulate the
perfection in divinity. They must always recognize that they
belong to an intermediary condition, highly circumscribed
and relatively brief in duration.

When Adam and Eve are thrust out of Eden, we may
imagine them weeping bitter tears—as in the paintings by
Masaccio or Michelangelo or Blake. They weep not only
because of remorse and a realization of how far they have
fallen from God's beneficent protectiveness, but also
because they intuit how frightening is the world into which
they have now been tossed. As yet, they do not know that
their awareness of good and evil has created in them a

special destiny not shared by anything else on earth. They have lost their innocence, but, without realizing it, they have acquired a creative spirit that will distinguish them from the rest of creation.

What preserves humanity in its permanent diaspora perforce appears objectively good to the descendants of Adam and Eve; and what threatens it must always seem bad. Because we want to live, death is to us an abomination that looms over every moment of our life. Furthermore, as *Genesis* implies, the world in which humanity must labor to survive is a penal settlement. God has chosen it as our punishment. But then how can we believe that this wretched existence may possibly be a consummation in itself, and death inherently evil?

We might reply that death is not an evil, and that life is not worth living if the good elements in our experience have disappeared completely, or been vastly outweighed by the bad ones. Should we infer from this that an enlightened spirit will have no feeling of repugnance toward its own annihilation? I doubt that this often happens. Consciousness in human beings achieves a level of introspection that views everything else in relation to itself as a constant, though changeable, entity that is programmed to pursue more and better life. Is it not reasonable to assume that this kind of being will treat its abolition as a tragedy of one sort or another?

Though this can tell us something about the phenomenology of spirit as it keeps on searching for its own consummation, we may still repudiate the suggestion that our death is always and necessarily tragic. We may agree that any death is a misfortune to the one who dies, in the sense that under optimal conditions he or she would probably want to live. But in our habitation outside the Garden of Eden, conditions are rarely optimal, and even at their relative best they inevitably deteriorate. The image of the Garden is itself just an abstract figment of what might have been but is not now. We must therefore approach these questions about the possible consummation of life, or the unavoidable tragedy of death, in a very different way.

How shall we go about it? Most people feel that the death of a young person, a youthful genius, let us say, is more tragic than the death of someone who is much older, even if that older person is also a genius. The death of Mozart, who died at the age of thirty-five, or Keats, who died at twenty-five, or others who are younger still, has a much greater effect on us than the deaths of Verdi or Tolstoy or many outstanding people who lived into their eighties. When we think of what Mozart and Keats were creating just before they died, we find it hard to believe that their talents had been fully consummated at that time in their lives. We may not be able to extrapolate beyond their life span and gauge with any accuracy what they might have achieved. But that just means that they had access to innovative capabilities that we cannot fathom whatever our stretch of imagination may be.

We can nevertheless feel confident that their attainments in the thirty or forty years of additional life they never had would have been astonishing. Until medical science changes the biological parameters of human existence, we have no reason to say the same about someone whose longevity has already exceeded theirs by four or five decades. We may lament the death of a Verdi or a Tolstoy, or for that matter anyone else of their age whom we care about. But in view of their diminished creativity, we would be unlikely to regard their demise as a *tragedy*.

The disparity in our sense of what is tragic in the life and death of different persons is therefore inversely proportionate to what we estimate as their unrealized potentialities. Because we think of Rossini as having largely fulfilled his musical promise during the first part of his life, after which his inventiveness remained more or less fallow for the next thirty years, his death at seventy-five seems like much less of a tragedy than the death of Schubert or Bizet, both of whom died in their early middle age.

Philosophers are mistaken when they claim that since almost everyone would like to live longer the advent of death must be an impending evil for each of us. To undermine this argument, we need only remember that death is more than just a termination. It is also a closure to the life that led up to it. Death is tragic or an evil if we have a great deal more to do in life, a great deal more that we want to do and are capable of doing, a great deal more that matters to us and that can possibly benefit either ourselves or others. Creative or merely imaginative men and women have a gift for augmenting the meaningfulness in life. That is why I initially chose artistic geniuses in my discussion of this issue. The tragedy or evil in their death seems clear to me. It negates the vibrancy of meaning that was still possible in them. Without that vibrancy, and to whatever extent it no longer exists, life is not worth living and its cessation is not a tragedy—though, of course, this itself may still be sad.

There are those who say that the misfortune of having to lose one's life is an evil, and therefore a sufficient reason to consider existence a tragedy for all finite creatures like ourselves. And if that is true, would not the death of any other person who has ever lived be just as tragic as the death of Keats? But this line of speculation cannot take us beyond the fact that it is unfortunate to be deprived of some good that one might have, above all when it is the good of being alive and the life one does have is a good life. From this alone, we cannot infer that death is equally tragic in every case, or inherently an evil.

The position I am criticizing maintains, in part, that chronological age at the time of death is irrelevant. That much I can agree to. The death of Keats was a tragedy not because he was twenty-five years old, but because he would have become an even greater poet than he was, and also a better and happier person, if he had a longer life. Had he been a soldier at a similar age who devoted his entire being to a cause for which he willingly died, we might think of his death as glorious and triumphant rather than tragic. We can regret that someone who distinguished himself as the soldier did should be deprived of life, but that is another matter. We may also feel aggrieved that anyone so young should have to die at all, but this too is beside the point.

In claiming that death is tragic for everyone, while also using Keats and Tolstoy as his examples, Thomas Nagel says: "If the normal lifespan were a thousand years, death at 80 would be a tragedy."[1] But the normal life span for human beings is not, and may never be, a thousand years. Empirical data such as this one elucidate constituents of what I have been calling the closure of a life. They establish the factual bases of our feelings and beliefs about the nature of our mortality. And even if people did go on for a thousand years, we might not conclude that death at eighty is at all tragic if the eighty year old was irremediably comatose or had a life of unbearable agony and no hope of ever profiting from continued life.

What matters most in our thinking about the consummation of life is the ability of a human being to have a meaningful existence, meaningfulness being geared to what this individual cares about and can possibly accomplish. It is not a question of our mere survival. In *The Death of Ivan Ilych*, Tolstoy says that his protagonist could imagine death happening to other men and women as a consequence of their mortality, but as applied to himself it made no sense at all. Nagel uses this reference to illustrate the difference between "internal" and "external" points of view. In her critique of Nagel, Mary Mothersill remarks that Ivan Ilych's attitude illustrates moral failure in him but not necessarily in everybody. She quotes from an essay in which Montaigne argues that people mistakenly think that their own death is more important or more unthinkable than the death of others.[2] Nagel and Mothersill both ignore the extent to which our response to death, whether our own or someone else's, varies in accordance with what is meaningful to us and to the world in which we live.

That is why we are so deeply affected by the death of those we love. These are people upon whom we have bestowed a great deal of value. We often have similar feelings when a leader or creative artist dies while still engaged in activities that manifest the vigor and strength of purpose that still functioned in him or her. We are staggered by the idea that life enhancement that has gone this far will not go any further. Where is the fertile mind that constantly astounded us? Where is the *person* we adored and admired, if only for the playfulness, the spontaneity, the animated spirit he or she still retained?

Tolstoy's novella examines this situation from a different perspective. Ivan Ilych is a commonplace individual distinguished only by his egocentric skills as a businessman. In dying as he does, however, he *becomes* exceptional. On his deathbed he concludes that his previous life was meaningless because he was out of touch with his reality. In treating death as something that happens to other people but not himself, he was guilty of self-deception. At the end, when he sees himself as a creature that dies because it is in its nature to do so, he outgrows illusions not only about immortality but also about his relative importance in life. He rises above his former egocentricity and comes to feel compassion for his wife and son, who must undergo the grief that his dying causes. The mystical revelation that Ivan Ilych finally experiences results from his recognition of what his way of existing had all along denied—his finitude and need for others.

In presenting this parable, Tolstoy conveys a paradoxical truth. Because Ivan Ilych manages to appreciate that no one has a special right to immortality, he achieves the self-awareness that can serve as a consummation of his life. His death is not an evil, or a tragedy, as it is for those whose lives we most admire. But he resembles them in having reached a level of spiritual elevation that few people attain, and that he could envisage only in his last moments. Though his death is not a tragic loss, it evokes feelings of pathos that may be comparable. Tolstoy makes us wonder what Ivan Ilych might have been like if he had had his revelation earlier in life. Possibly a greater man, whose death would *then* have been a tragedy?

The naturalist perspective upon consummation that I am sketching is not entirely different from the one that Aristotle presupposes in his ideas about human happiness (*eudaemonia*). He defines happiness as fulfillment of the faculties that adapt us to the world that we inhabit. In Raphael's painting *The School of Athens* Aristotle gestures with a horizontal hand in contrast to Plato, who points upward. Nevertheless, Aristotle extolled rationality as the *highest* of our faculties. He thought that virtue and the integrity of life must be understood in terms of consummate reason. From this there followed all of the elitism and class stratification in Aristotle's political theory. He idealized Athenian society, despite its latent hostility toward philosophers, because he thought it was the only one in which reason's importance for the good life had been accorded even superficial recognition.

Aristotle misunderstood the way in which reason contributes to the good life. Reason is not the absolute or ultimate consummation of our being. It is only one among other human capabilities that can yield, within their limitations and if all goes well, consummatory experience. Though reason has instrumental utility for survival and consequent enjoyment, it is not a final terminus of value. It is an aspect of life that can be rewarding in itself, in its regulative principles and native modes of inference, some of which it alone creates, and for reasons of its own. But there is no justification for maintaining that unaided rationality evinces the validity or underlying meaning that ethics and religion can then promulgate as the resolution of the human predicament. To approach either affective or cognitive matters as Aristotle does is to succumb to a grotesque dream about the nature of reason. That is not the same as living with its reality.

In making this remark, I have in mind Goya's painting *El sueño de la razón produce monstruos*. The word *sueño* being ambiguous, the title is sometimes translated as *The Sleep of Reason produces Monsters* and sometimes as *The Dream of Reason produces Monsters*. We observe a man lying across a desk with his eyes closed and his head resting on his arm. Fearful creatures and dark deformities fill his room as representations of the evils that invade his slumber. That much is presented in the painting. But what is the meaning of its title? Most commentators have thought it signifies that monstrosities enter the human mind when reason sleeps and dreaming takes charge. If, in our psychoanalytic sophistication, we identify the content of dreams with the ravaging unconscious in everyone, we may also conclude that reason is needed to bring to the surface of awareness the dismal tendencies that always lurk within human affect.

I see the picture differently. I interpret the title as meaning that reason *itself* generates the distorted figures that surround the sleeping individual. The scene is a showing forth of reason's baleful dream, a depiction of what reason fabricates when it tyrannizes over the mentality of men and women, when it mangles emotional sensibilities that are ingrained in us and require consummation that reason diabolically denies. Those are the horrors Goya portrays, horrors that are greater than anything unbridled passion might perpetrate, since reason is able to mobilize them through hideous systems of vicious ideology.

When Aristotle exiled himself from Athens because he feared that it might sin a second time against philosophy, in other words, that it might put him to death as it had previously done with Socrates, he took the easy way out of an ethical situation that Socrates confronted with greater heroism in refusing to run away. It is a dilemma moral philosophers must study, but also one that concerns the nature of philosophy itself and its self-presentation. In Plato's consecutive portrait of him, Socrates appears as an ironist. He is a man who says the opposite of what he thinks in order to convey most effectively the truth of what he believes. As Dr. Johnson put it, irony of this type is a "mode of speech in which the meaning is contrary to the words."[3]

That is how one must interpret the various claims of ignorance that Socrates makes on occasions when he tries to elicit agreement about a moral truth he does not doubt at all.

In the earlier dialogues of Plato, devoted to illustrations of his master at work, Socrates repeatedly denies that he is wise or has any extraordinary knowledge. In his professed uncertainty about how to live, he probes the abstrusities encased in our ideas about the good life. He defends his manner of approach by citing the oracle at Delphos that called him the wisest man in Athens, although he himself says he knows nothing. Socrates finally suspects that the oracle, talking poetically as usual, meant that in relation to fundamental questions only he knows that he does not know. With this bit of clarification, Socrates can then proceed in the right direction, searching for truths that everyone seeks but that elude those who begin with the false assurance that they know what in fact they do not know.

In these early dialogues, and in most of the later ones, Socrates is never a solitary thinker. He does not carry out his investigations in his head. Far from being a man who deals with philosophical problems privately, on his own, he is always shown conversing with others. They meet in the agora, often by chance, and discuss moral and political matters that are hard to understand or resolve. Socrates can lead the inquiries that ensue because he knows he does not know and yet has faith in his methodology. As it develops, it becomes a logic, an *elenchus*, that helps to cleanse our thinking and exclude unacceptable types of inference.

The logic that Socrates invents is an artifact of intellect. It is reason and analysis without which there can be no philosophy, or science, or any other intelligent pursuit of a life worth living. But in denying that he has a special and supreme kind of knowledge, Socrates subordinates the rationality without which he could not function. He uses it as a tool for his service to the community, and as part of the communication among human beings which exists when he talks to fellow Athenians about good or bad realities of their situation. The social circumstance of his method is not just a stage setting, a cardboard background for what he does in his logic. It is integral to the very doing of logical or philosophical inquiry as he imaginatively performs it.

When Socrates succeeds in this creative venture, he achieves more than just the consummation of his powers as an intellectual. He also conveys what it is to be a person of his time and place, an individual living with others who are jointly beset by issues they must disentangle through their combined efforts as cooperative investigators. While he insists, in his ironic way, that he has nothing to teach, Socrates takes command of each discussion. He instructs others in the search of truths that he intuits but they must discover for themselves. The ability to live fruitfully despite the doubt, the uncertainty, and the emotional as well as mental difficulty of this effort is itself a consummation of our humanity that cannot be achieved in any other manner.

For this reason, Socrates was the first great humanist in philosophy while also being the father of rigorous analysis that is crucial in the doing of anything truly philosophical. If his arguments throughout the Platonic dialogues seem technically deficient, as they often are, we can easily ignore this flaw since rationality itself was only secondary in his attempt to find and to exemplify what is distinctive of our species when it grapples with its moral problems.

The imaginative quest that Socrates enacts, and idealizes inasmuch as he dedicates so much of his life to it, is arduous in more than one respect. Not only must the effort be carried out with honesty and precision, but also it becomes a threat to those who enjoy the lulling sustenance of dogmatic verities. These can be handed down from generation to generation; they can be institutionalized in traditional religions or bureaucracies and rigid legal codes. The humanistic vocation that Socrates represents has to be reborn, reinvented, in each person who devotes his or her talents to it. The philosophy Socrates embodies is an art form, a living art using ideas as its materials and relying on skills that are affective as well as cognitive, intuitive and interpersonal as well as inductive or deductive. Few people have the capacity to savor the aesthetic consummations of this art. And many of those who are endowed with the requisite aptitude misconstrue its character or resent the laborious commitment it entails.

In a society that does not respect the liberal approach to free inquiry that Socratic methodology fosters, this art can seem threatening, even subversive, perhaps treasonous. Battered by their failures in the Peloponnesian War, for some of which Socrates's pupils were to blame, the Athenian public was in no mood to tolerate anyone who dared to inspect the received opinions of their society. Had the Athenians quickly vanquished their enemies and maintained an empire as they wished, they might have ignored an old gadfly who had served the state in previous years. Having instead reached the end of their military rope, they could perceive him only as a disquieting and defiantly abusive irritant. They thought that putting him to death would end his deleterious influence.

In a sense the Athenians who condemned Socrates were right, as he himself intimates in his nonapologetic *Apology*. The aspect of human nature for which he sought an adequate fulfillment runs counter to, and in time of emergency may well seem inimical toward, automatic acceptance of whatever banal notions have been nurtured in each citizen. The conventional ideas about the gods, and about the Athenian virtues they symbolized, were explicit guidelines for well-bred youths. In reeducating his tutees, Socrates disrupted all that. The results could only be ruinous.

In the arrogance of his final self-defense, Socrates overtly courts disaster. Like Alceste in Molière's *The Misanthrope*, he might have wanted to lose his case "pour la beauté du fait," for the beauty of it. By revealing the corruption in those who dared to punish him for being a vehicle of civic consummation, a savior of what is most deeply human and Athenian, he would be getting them to show themselves as they really are. There is an aesthetic finesse in this maneuver, one that Socrates the ironist might well have relished. His detractors were unable to appreciate it.

Moreover, the human spirit evolves in ways that can defeat intentions such as theirs. Socrates predicted that he would become a martyr, but even he could not have known how greatly his mission would enlarge itself throughout the centuries. His adversaries were soon forgotten, though subsequent philosophers have noted shortcomings in his thinking that even his contemporary critics discerned and that we should not ignore. Jeremy Bentham, revolted by the conservative and blatantly reactionary ethics that Socrates professed, condemned him as one who "talked nonsense under the pretense of teaching wisdom and morality."[4] But more challenging, and possibly more devastating, is the attack that Nietzsche launched against the Socratic outlook.

In *The Birth of Tragedy* Nietzsche argues that Socrates both represents and contributes to the demise of Greek art. The spirit that had motivated it, notably in the work of tragedians such as Aeschylus and Sophocles, Nietzsche ascribes to what he calls the Dionysian attitude toward life. This combines adherence to metaphysical pessimism with acceptance of vital impulse underlying the creativity that gives life its value. When it also accommodates a contrary interest in beauty and elegance, which Nietzsche terms the

Apollonian, he considers the Dionysian approach inspirational in all great art, tragedy and music in particular. He traces the decline of Greek tragedy to the work of Euripides, the friend and follower of Socrates.

Nietzsche depicts Socratism as protoscientistic reliance on logic and clarity of thought, naive confidence about the attainability of knowledge, and faith in the optimistic shibboleth that conscious self-awareness is preferable to any form of instinctual abandon. Ignoring the fact that even the wildest instinct can be molded into art, Socratism could only constitute an intellectualized collapse of Athenian culture. Far from regarding Socrates as a guide to the secrets of human nature, Nietzsche sees him as a beginning of the wrong turn that Western philosophy has followed ever since.

Sixteen years after he wrote *The Birth of Tragedy* Nietzsche added a new preface in which he harshly criticized some of his book's main ideas. But he retained his initial stance on Socratism and what he thought to be its erroneous claims about dispassionate reasoning: "Might it not be that the 'inquiring mind' was simply the human mind terrified by pessimism and trying to escape from it, a clever bulwark erected against the truth? . . . Had this perhaps been your secret, great Socrates? Most secretive of ironists, had this been your deepest irony?"[5]

As often happens with Nietzsche, the truth he ferrets out and illuminates so brilliantly is only a partial truth. In the Socratic view of life there is indeed a cooling of those instincts and spontaneous impulses that Nietzsche idealized. The consummations Socrates offers are not the ones that Nietzsche proclaims. To say, however, that Socrates wanted to throttle the Dionysian or deprive it of its power to further creativity is to miss entirely what he recommended. Like Nietzsche himself, Socrates was a

moral philosopher who tried to duplicate the achievement
of great artists, in music and tragedy among other aesthetic
vehicles, by formulating a view of life itself as art. At its most
accomplished, the good life was for him a compendium of
various consummations, some that emanate from logic and
conceptual exploration but also others that pertain to
Dionysian as well as Apollonian attitudes in religion or
morality. His adherents in the succeeding millennia have
differently emphasized one or another of the two elements.
The varying achievements of these disciples were
predicated upon a similar hope that the example of Socrates
would liberate humankind from blind submission to
fallacious beliefs and the unexamined narrowness of
mindless society.

Is this Socratic point of view less, or possibly more,
constructive than the one that Nietzsche advocates? For
some artistic media it might well be harmful. At a moment
in Greek history when tragedy had already reached its
apogee, Socratic thought may have symbolized or even
accelerated the impending deterioration of the drama. But
art forms are always in a state of evolution, the older dying
out while new ones take their place. Human imagination is
not infinite in its capability, and what awakens it may
sometimes survive only by deflecting aesthetic energy away
from inspirational possibilities that mattered to earlier
generations. The greatness of Socrates consisted in his
creating a systematic art of life that filled a space in Western
self-construction that had been left undeveloped before.
Socrates *lived* that art, as if his everyday routine were itself
a quasi-comedic satyr play that followed upon the works of
all the tragedians and delivered a viable answer to the
painful questions they had raised.

Nietzsche calls Socrates the epitome of the "theoretical"
man. That is correct, since Socrates was a philosopher

forever trying to discover theories that could reveal the truth. But his love of the truth, and his belief that nothing must be allowed to prevent us from seeking it, was not itself theoretical. It was an affective disposition that becomes consummatory by creating thoughts in one who has the essential courage and capacity. By extending the imaginative scope of this secular religion through unflinching discourse with those who would join him in discussion, Socrates attained a life that was significant as well as meaningful.

Nietzsche was right in asserting that ceaseless optimism pervaded the Socratic project. It was faith in the possibility of living well despite any pessimistic metaphysics that we might also accept. To this extent, it was yea-saying and a will to power that Nietzsche could have applauded instead of condemning. The deepest of Socrates's ironies is not the avoidance of frightening ideas about the universe but rather the buoyant willingness to speculate about them as conceivably correct and yet as vanquished by our ability to face their catastrophic implications with steadfast honesty. This too is a consummation of our being which cannot result from any other response.

When John Stuart Mill dealt with consummation as the basis of human happiness, he reverted to the hedonism he culled from his father, from Bentham, and from their antecedents in the eighteenth century. He did so because he, like them, considered pleasure an obvious touchstone of natural completions. It was present at some time or other in the experience of everyone, and it signified good health in the organism that had it. Because he thought pleasure was quantifiable, Bentham devised a hedonic calculus that might enable scientists to determine why and how people make affective choices. Mill rejected the calculus, and possibly hedonism itself, once he decided that this approach ignored the fact of qualitative differences. His own solution, in terms of authoritative critics who have personal knowledge of alternate pleasures and can therefore decide judiciously which are higher or lower in quality, was offered as a criterion for discovering authentic and thoroughly human consummations. These would give meaning to the idea of greatest happiness, or even greatest pleasure, provided that "greatest" was understood to entail whatever the qualified judges preferred in view of their own experience.

Mill took this position in philosophy because he wanted to construct an ethics that recognizes the validity of altruistic as well as selfish feelings. The latter seeks organic and usually preprogrammed consummations that his scientifically oriented predecessors had treated as the universal motives of behavior. But Mill knew that sympathetic and compassionate attachments are also innate in our species. By fitting them into the naturalistic framework he inherited and wished to refine, Mill thought he could show that the consummations they induce must be accepted as supplementing, on a higher qualitative plane, those that mere selfishness can offer.

By means of this compromise Mill wished to retain the vestiges of hedonism while also incorporating moral attitudes—social concern, humanitarian kindliness, even self-sacrifice—that are praiseworthy whether or not they afford much pleasure. His decision procedure for what is better or worse in human experience could thus include the belief that these consummations are somehow comparable to the ones that predominate in our self-oriented responses and can be investigated scientifically.

Assuming I have not misread Mill's view, how acceptable is it as philosophy? I feel it was a major mistake on his part. Compassion and all the other nonselfish attachments may be explained and possibly justified as consummatory syndromes, but the consummations they produce are structurally different from those that issue from the selfishness Mill and his forebears deemed characteristic of human nature. In this question, Mill is as much of a reductivist as Bentham or even Freud. Since science has had great success in relating the selfish areas of affectivity to organic satisfactions useful for the biological survival of an individual, or of a group, these thinkers infer that consummations across the spectrum of attachments must be alike in that respect.

But this convoluted assumption cripples the naturalistic position that science rightly wants to promote. It ignores what is obvious. Though the hero facing death on the ramparts of a noble cause experiences a consummation of something in his very being, it would be foolhardy to think that he attains the goodness that pleasures of the flesh, or of the purposive intellect, might have given him. These are different kinds of consummation. They are not alike, and no criteria of quantification or of qualified judges can give one a universal and reliable means of choosing among them. Here as elsewhere, reductivism defeats the truth of whatever promising intuitions may have fathered it.

The dangers of such reductivism are strewn like roadblocks throughout Freud's remarks about affective attachments. They are injurious to his ideas not only about love and altruism or compassion but also about sexuality. Having criticized his theories in several books, I would like to focus here on one that has major importance in the field of gender studies which is now growing rapidly. Just as Freud reduces love to aim-inhibited sexuality, and compassionate responses of every sort to devious but generally misguided interest in what is advantageous for oneself, so too does he reduce sexual instinct to libidinal energy that scarcely recognizes, and even blurs, the differences between male and female.

Without denying the implications of anatomical disparity between the sexes, Freud seems to hold that sexual impulse is directed toward consummation that remains in principle the same regardless of the gender of whatever individual who elicits it. On the one hand, he maintains that libido is impelled toward heterosexual coitus that can eventuate in the reproduction of the species, which means that polymorphous indulgence or homosexuality among adults must always be a perversion of the instinct; on the other hand, he considers bisexuality to be the human norm, since libido can seek, and be satisfied by, objects of desire that are indiscriminately male or female.

In the decades since Freud presented this theory of bisexuality, his suggestion has received wide agreement even among people who reject the rest of his thinking. It has been treated as a truism in literary criticism as well as psychology. An interesting case history in this regard is Thomas Mann's celebrated novella *Death in Venice*. That is a story about a famous author, Gustav Aschenbach, who travels south from Munich hoping to recover in Venice from physical and emotional fatigue. Though he has never before had an attachment to a person of his own gender, he becomes infatuated with a beautiful fourteen-year-old boy, Tadzio, whom he does not speak to or touch.

Writing in 1911, Mann fills the narrative with sexual ambiguities that occur throughout all his writings. Is Aschenbach's interest homosexual, albeit largely repressed in view of his prior history as a straight and conventional married man? Since his obsessiveness is portrayed as an affliction, a moral degradation that exposes him to the cholera epidemic and causes his death, does it signify bisexuality that is basically pathological? If so, can no such relationship be healthy and truly consummatory? Or are both of these alternatives real possibilities, each contingent upon personal development and the social rearing of the people involved?

In his dramatic and ironic fashion, Mann makes little attempt to resolve these ambiguities. He emphasizes the fact that Aschenbach is a disciplined and dedicated artist, a writer with strict literary standards. Being a purist devoted to the beauties of artistic form, Aschenbach has neglected the pleasures of passionate indulgence as well as the calmer delights of sensuous enjoyment. Initially at least, he is fascinated by Tadzio because he sees him as an embodiment of the perfection one finds in Greek statuary. Later he feels a paternal protectiveness toward the boy. But eventually his inability to turn away from this attachment becomes destructive to himself as an artist and as a human being.

Without being overly didactic, Mann links Aschenbach's experience to the reflections about love that occur in Plato's *Phaedrus*. Socrates there discusses erotic attachment in terms of problems that all artists face. He argues that the artistic soul must satisfy two prerequisites: it must search for beauty and it must do so through formal, even abstract principles definitive of an aesthetic medium.

According to Socrates, these two demands are in conflict with each other. He maintains that an artist can perceive the beautiful only as it appears to the senses and is enclosed within a conglomeration of particular attributes belonging to things or persons that comprise the world of phenomena. Without immersing themselves in that world, artists cannot find the essence of beauty that they seek. If, however, in their eagerness to reach their ideal goal, they fixate on some arresting manifestation of the beautiful, they are dazzled and run the risk of failing in their chosen mission.

But it would be equally dangerous, Socrates continues, if an artist imposes an exceptionally severe discipline upon himself. Such artificial restraints are likely to cause a repressed but explosive condition that may also culminate in self-indulgence, undermining the artist's love of beauty and causing moral or even bodily calamity. In the *Phaedrus*, Socrates leaves the issue there. He does not offer a decisive answer to it.

Far from doing so himself, Mann introduces a speech of Socrates that does not exist in the Platonic dialogue and that is much more extreme in the alternatives it depicts. The wording in Mann's passage makes it sound as if Socrates thought that there can be no happy resolution to the problem he has posed. In that event the tragedy of Aschenbach's death in Venice must be taken as a venomous reality that resides beneath the surface of *all* artistic effort. This pessimistic conclusion is coherent with Mann's belief, drawn from his reading in Freud and Schopenhauer, that art is a product of disease that sensitive people cultivate in themselves for the sake of perceiving beauty and sometimes creating it.

Death in Venice is instructive not only because it awakens queries about the beautiful as a consummatory good but also because it directs these queries to a situation in which the appetite for beauty fosters troublesome attachments that are presumably induced by human bisexuality. Recent biographers claim that in this writing, and in his life, Mann was concerned about the nature of his sexual feelings toward other men.[6] Several critics have insisted that to understand the novella properly one must know that Mann was actively homosexual, while also being conventionally heterosexual in his long and stable marriage.[7]

But the evidence adduced for these assertions is convincing only if we think that love directed toward someone of one's own gender is invariably based upon homosexuality that is either latent or explicit, either repressed or carried to carnal intercourse. If we reject that presupposition, we end up with very different views about *Death in Venice* as well as the personal experience that the author has expressed by means of it.

In the novella some details do suggest a libidinal interest on Aschenbach's part. Near the end, having contracted the cholera infection that will shortly kill him, he has a nightmare that includes an orgiastic sequence. In it his wild and frantic behavior may be taken as having partly homosexual intent. But once we relinquish the Freudian dogma about bisexuality as a universal key to consummation between people of the same sex, we need not give this episode undue importance or interpret the entire narrative, and its relevance to the artistic temperament, from a predominantly gay perspective.

Mann might have got the idea for his story during a chance encounter with Gustav Mahler. On a train returning home after an Italian sojourn, Mahler is said to have described a sexual adventure he had in Venice with a very young girl. Her age was a part of what made the anecdote so entrancing in Mann's imagination. By changing the gender of the beloved, his novella avoids any conflict with the established taboo about abuse of little girls, while also capitalizing upon the forbidden, and equally titillating, intimation of pedophilia for a boy.

In eliminating the banal details of Mahler's account, the latter tactic would be preferable for a story about a staid and unerotic disciplinarian's search for absolute beauty. Mann obviously wanted to meld the anecdotal occurrence into a broader, more penetrating study of consummations available to the creative soul. Aschenbach never accosts the boy whose beauty has enthralled him. He looks and follows him but—as far as we can tell—he experiences little or nothing that might suggest libidinal desire (except in the orgiastic dream). The attachment, such as it is, depends upon other interests and other kinds of fulfillment.

From the very start we are told that Aschenbach had enjoyed a brief period of happiness with his wife, who is now dead. She bore him a daughter, still living, but "a son he never had." Aschenbach hovers over the handsome though sickly boy with a kind of paternal love he might have felt toward his own child. When he learns that there is an epidemic in Venice, Aschenbach feels an obligation to alert the boy's mother. He neglects to do so, however, since he dreads the possibility of being left without the daily presence of Tadzio. He thereby fails to achieve the consummation of his humane and fatherly feelings toward this surrogate son.

Furthermore, Aschenbach has been described to us in the early pages as an author who has sought aesthetic excellence throughout his life. Being a creator of beauty in the formal patterns for which his writings have become famous, he would naturally be intrigued by a relationship that exists only at a distance and through the balletic play of visual imagination. The unapproachability of Tadzio enables Aschenbach to love him as he does. Once this love degenerates into a self-destructive obsession, we see how easily the pursuit of beauty can lead an artist into the abyss—just as Socrates said.

But neither the pursuit nor the abyss itself has to be construed as fundamentally sexual. Nor must either be taken to signify homosexuality on the part of the story's author. One of the biographies to which I referred mentions an occasion, during a stay at a seaside resort in the company of his family, when Mann attentively watched a small and pampered ten-year-old boy playing on the beach. Mann doubtless saw in him something he could use as a novelist. We have no reason to take his behavior as evidence of what the biographer loosely calls "homoeroticism."

A great deal of Mann's genius consisted in his talent for acute observation. It enabled him to invoke a sense of realism and verisimilitude that supports his fictional inquiries into human motivation. To look and to see perceptively is itself a consummation of much that is distinctively human. This type of consummation strengthens and sustains the further consummations afforded by imagination and our sense of beauty. In a description of a handsome boy that he happened to see one day, Mann reports that his interest in this youth was nothing but an "aesthetic . . . inclination, the goal of which, it would appear, is realized in gazing and 'admiring.' Although erotic, it requires no fulfillment at all, neither intellectually nor physically."[8] Through his writing Mann transformed that perceptual interest into something that makes art a source of value and an agency of spirit.

I return to this idea in the next chapter. Here I want to examine further the nature of Aschenbach's love, and what it may tell us about Mann himself. The novella is a study in the perils of seeking to achieve what Mann calls "high humanity." These words occur in a letter in which he rejects as follows the misconstrual of his work: "That mature masculinity reaches out its arm, showing itself to be tender towards masculinity which is softer and more beautiful—I find in this nothing unnatural and a great deal that is edifying, a great deal of high humanity."[9] That alone, as a goal anyone may pursue, either through sexuality or without it, is an adequate and sufficient explanation of the psychodynamic elements in this kind of attachment.

Mann's remark that I have quoted is reminiscent of Oscar Wilde's statement to the jury that imprisoned him for engaging in homosexual conduct. Though Wilde was guilty as charged, his portrayal of "the 'love' that dare not speak its name in this century" enunciates an elevated conception similar to the one Mann described in his letter. That love, Wilde affirmed, "is such a great affection of an older for a younger man as there was between David and Jonathan, such as Plato made the very base of his philosophy and such as you find in the sonnets of Michelangelo and Shakespeare—a deep spiritual affection that is as pure as it is perfect and dictates great works of art like those of Shakespeare and Michelangelo. . . . It is beautiful; it is fine; it is the noblest form of affection. It is intellectual, and it repeatedly exists between an elder and a younger man, when the elder man has intellect, and the younger man has all the joy, hope and glamour of life."[10]

Finally I turn to a paragraph toward the beginning of the narrative that clearly reveals the degree to which Aschenbach's love of Tadzio is not sexual. The passage associates their acts of mutual observation with a need, present in all strangers who happen to be thrown together, to recognize and regard each other as a fellow creature that one might often see but never meet. Mann asserts that "one human being instinctively feels respect and love for another human being, so long as he does not know him well enough to judge him."[11]

Whether or not this generalization is defensible, it pertains to affective attachment in search of consummations that cannot be subsumed within sexuality itself, in this instance either bisexuality or latent homosexuality. Useful as those concepts may be under circumscribed conditions, they do not have the facile applicability frequently assigned to them. In relation to *Death in Venice*, which I have picked as a case study because it is so challenging, the idea that the sought-for consummations must be either explicitly or subterraneously libidinal is both tendentious and misleading.[12]

Mann's story lends itself to the interpretation I find dubious because, in its ironic presentation, the plot draws upon a reality that is often not at all ambiguous: an older man watching the movements of a beautiful boy in the hope that genital pleasures may eventually ensue. But since a same-sex attachment can transcend, or at least eschew, sexual overtones of this sort, it encourages us to reconsider the ways in which bonding within a single gender may be geared to consummations that are neither physical nor especially sex-related.

Freud misunderstood these extrasexual tropes of human nature. Throughout his group psychology, he claims that it is the energy of aim-inhibited sexuality that unites intimate friends, closely compatible colleagues, soldiers fighting jointly in an army, members of a society collectively engaged, people excited by a common cause, and fellow enthusiasts in the same religion or philanthropic enterprise. The aim that is being inhibited Freud considers sexual in the libidinal sense of that word. When participants in these relations are of the same gender, and above all when they feel love for each other, the respective consummations would have to originate in latent homosexuality.

This conceptual step is, however, a leap in the dark. Even if we believe that sexual instinct, possibly sexual feeling as well, is somehow present in all human experience, we have no reason to think that it has more than a minor effect upon most attachments in society. As we may use the word *love* to designate attitudes of compassion and the willingness to accept another's indefeasible right to live, so too we may speak of friends feeling love for each other without there being any suggestion of bisexuality in either of them.

Nonsexual love can be taken as what it seems to be—an earnest, and often deeply felt, dedication to some other person, or to the goals one shares with him or her. The same applies to the many other affective attachments that life in society initiates and encourages. To appreciate the nature of each particular relationship we would have to evaluate the character, the duration, the quantity, and the quality of whatever bestowals and appraisals make it what it is.

Love can exist without there being significant elements of any sexuality, whether libidinal, romantic, or explicitly erotic. In an attenuated form, the erotic probably pervades our existence, and in friendly or social conditions that have nothing to do with reproductive impulse it is most likely to occur throughout. Yet love cannot be defined in terms of it alone. Nor is the erotic isomorphic with love. In their relations to each other, they vary widely as motivational vectors from one moment to the next.[13]

Seen from this perspective, the greatness of Mann's achievement in *Death in Venice* and his other fiction takes on a different coloration. Aschenbach's love of Tadzio, and Mann's own love for men throughout his life, can then be interpreted as entirely coherent with his repeated denials of homosexual intentions in this story about an artist's tragic search for beauty and idealistic love. Mann agreed with Nietzsche's remark that "The degree and kind of a man's sexuality permeate the loftiest heights of his intellect."[14] But neither Mann nor Nietzsche believed that these loftiest heights are just a sublimation of the sexuality that permeates them.

In Mann's own life, even the feelings of love for Paul Ehrenberg and for Klaus Heiser that he mentions in his *Diaries* elude a typical Freudian interpretation. Referring to the first, he speaks of "the wild surges of exultation and deep despair of that central emotional experience at twenty-five." He says that love of that kind "has happened only once in my life, which is doubtless as it should be." The second occasion, years afterward, he characterizes as "a late surprise, with a quality of benign fulfillment about it."[15]

The passionate attachment in these relations may well have been sexual in some sense of that word, and, for all we know, it might have yielded libidinal consummations. Entries in Mann's final diaries, in which he records his infatuation with Franz Westermeier, a young waiter whom he found attractive, suggest the possibility of masturbatory phantasies in relation to him. The question that some commentators find so intriguing—did Mann have sex with persons of the same gender?—is of secondary importance. The love that he felt for these and possibly other men, and that he wrote about with such provocative insight, is not reducible to any physical dimension and incorporates much that is not itself physical.

Here as in general, Freud favored his reductivistic view because it has an elegance that he prized throughout his theory construction. He believed it explains what might otherwise appear to be hopelessly unformulatable. He could not accept the possibility that the appearance is actually faithful to reality. But life defeats Freud's formulation. A pluralistic approach is inevitably more cumbersome than his, and sometimes matted over with complexities that thwart our craving for hidden essentialistic truths. Nevertheless, the Freudian approach is not preferable. Though reductivism may be flattering to our pigeonholing intellect, the world is more fluidly diverse than theorists like Freud have been willing to admit.

Instead of squeezing into a single box the multitude of possible consummations that people pursue in their social being, we should realize that these consummations, offsprings of varied imagination and idealization, differ among themselves to a larger extent than anything we can readily categorize. The consummatory goods of intimate friendship or fervent public service or intense religious affiliation have unique characteristics of their own. Sexual reductivism does not help us to appreciate and coherently promote these consummations, whether they result from individual needs or social mandates, from interpersonal bonds or humanitarian sentiments and group solidarities.

In our age mankind has taken momentous strides toward the freedom to recognize and enjoy an array of fully sexual interests. Nothing more is gained by doctrinal insistence that all other types of consummation must somehow be dependent upon them.[16]

Since art is designed to induce consummations coherent with, and dependent upon, the techniques of some medium, many works of art could be used to substantiate my reflections in this chapter. In the West we have been inundated by aesthetic productions that take as their subject matter sexual and amorous attachments. Though their public may have erotic or romantic longings for literary figments as varied as Julien Sorel in *The Red and the Black* and Dorothea Brook in *Middlemarch*, the proffered consummations are not often libidinal or overtly sexual. Even the most thorough description of such intriguing characters leaves much to the reader's idiosyncratic imagination. The author's skill consists in making available a framework of possibilities that must be given surrogate actuality by each individual in the audience as an extension of his or her prior experience. Living in this vicarious manner through affective situations that belong to the narrative, the reader acquires a derivative consummation, a reconstruction at second hand of what the author has imagined. Without this leveraged bond, uniting the imaginations of artist and recipient, no communication— aesthetic or nonaesthetic—will occur between them.

The emergent consummations of which I speak must not be confused with the happy daydreams or delightful fantasies that people may also obtain from art, particularly narrative literature. We do not have to be a psychiatrist to know that men and women use nonexistent persons as replacements for the real ones they would like to love, or make love to, but cannot for whatever reason. This is a well-established truth about wish fulfillment as an ersatz goodness that can be garnered from works of art. But more significant, I think, is the fact that no fictional character, however suitable for love or suggestive as a sexual object, can have its effect upon members of an audience unless, to paraphrase Shakespeare, they upon their imaginary forces work. As I show at greater length in the next chapter, this is an aesthetic phenomenon that yields its own inclusive values.

Through its creative capability, artistic employment of imagination takes on a function and consequent meaning very different from the satisfying of repressed desires and thwarted impulses. Aesthetic consummation depends not on sublimation, but rather on someone's direct response to the imaginative form and content of a work. That turns even the most pressing of sexual or interpersonal urgencies into feelings that are enjoyable as transformations of reality. They are not duplications of anything. The resultant gratifications are usually far removed from those that our organic yearnings seek. Aesthetic consummations are nevertheless cognate as fulfillments: they too reveal how finely tuned is our human ability to activate and deploy the vital energy of our being as affective entities.

My idea will become pellucid if we change the medium under consideration from the literary to the filmic or operatic. Though pornography has long existed as a subdivision of literature, its goal is better served by arts like cinema. Since written pornography must be read and therefore subsumed within a more deliberative process, it is readily deflected from its aim of arousing the physical reactions that comprise sexual response. If, however, the titillating behavior and exposure of naked flesh need only be seen, observed in a visual presentation as if we were ourselves located where the camera is, the consummation of purely sexual urges can succeed with greater impact.

People who condemn X-rated movies on moral grounds may have trouble persuading us about the harmfulness of these films. But scruples about their artistic merit are easier to defend. Because pornographic movies usually exclude the subtle consummations that result from imaginative awareness of the personal and social realities sex involves, these movies rarely avail themselves of the fullest range of aesthetic possibilities. This has generally been true of literary pornography as well, but the deficiency is accentuated by the quasi-voyeuristic power of film.

Consummation in cinematic experience as a whole is enriched, not lessened, by our knowledge that the two-dimensional representations of humanity that we perceive on screen have only limited resemblance to reality as we know it. The characters look like real men or women and yet affect us differently. Though a crowd scene gives us the feeling of being in the midst of living people, we are always conscious of our distance from them. Film art is artificial, like all other arts, but since its techniques include so many violations of normal vision they have an augmented capacity to detach us from the world of actuality. In doing so, they are able to elicit a vague but persistent feeling that we ourselves control our affective affiliations to what is actual in that world. And in that event, are we not empowered to consummate, if only in this unreal situation, our many interests in it?

When pornography softens its goal-orientation, or lingers through exploratory means of purveying sexual pleasure, it becomes erotic art worthy of having a reputable niche in filmmaking. It then affords consummations of our desire to live among human beings with healthy interests that are communicative as well as assertive, nonphysical as well as genital, interpersonal as well as appetitive and self-oriented. Despite, or possibly because of, its mechanized artificiality, cinematic art can accommodate superbly these variant types of consummation.

Opera and vocal music as a whole are unlike film inasmuch as their fictions are usually staged and generally unrealistic. But though the singers and other performers produce their art within the artificial confines of a theater, or as soloists accompanied by orchestral instruments assembled for this purpose, they show forth reality in being alive and real themselves. They appear before us with the kind of immediacy that actors in a play also have. They are right there, making their performance as we watch and listen to them. In the film experience we literally see only images. In opera we see men and women carrying out a role that relies upon the specialized talents they display to us.

This mixture of the aesthetic and the actual in a musical production is an extremely fertile resource for consummatory possibilities. They are realized through the sonic impact of operatic music. Though opera is also a visual art, it subordinates that aspect of its medium. In doing so, however, it has to limit its ability to copy what people are like in their natural circumstance. Film does not have a comparable problem in its mode of representation. Moreover opera always runs the risk of seeming ridiculous. No one in the everyday world sings so constantly.

Opera deals with such difficulties by making a virtue of its dilemma. Since people do not vocalize their way through life as they do in opera, and since they do not depend upon accompanists who elaborate their every utterance, the lyric mode invites its audience to participate in its artful fictionality by responding to the expressiveness of harmonic and melodic sounds. The distinctive consummations in opera result from its capacity to transform affect as it ordinarily exists into musically satisfying expressions of it. This involves something more than just a revelation of interpersonal or social feelings. That much can be achieved by plays or other nonmusical performances in a theater. In opera there is an additional dimension that is crucial to its inventiveness, namely, the continual presence of music that magnifies the affect. The expressive sounds in opera are louder and more explicit than those we hear anywhere else. The feelings that imbue these sounds are systematically enlarged, and often simplified for the sake of instant awareness and enjoyment.

As a result, the music that yields operatic consummations is only partly programmatic. Though much of it is iconic or parallel to what is happening in the dramaturgy, operatic music functions in ways that are more elusive. Not even the composer will always know how to describe in words the specific feelings that his or her work expresses. Only on occasion does the music attempt to be an isomorphic representation of something. Instead the artist presents a quasi-metaphoric template of sounds that may awaken in the audience a responsiveness based upon their perception of what the characters are feeling. Great music for the opera is a distillation and not an absolute correspondence to what we encounter anywhere in life. It redirects our normal searching for emotional completion into a musico-dramatic vehicle that yields its particular type of gratification. Its peculiar combination of artificial delights puts opera and its allied media in a class of their own.

Something similar applies to nonvocal music as well. The aesthetic opportunities that come from using dramatic and even quasi-programmatic effects in works that are not operatic were perfectly understood by Mozart. At the end of his life, he wrote orchestral compositions—for instance, the last symphonies and piano concertos—that contain the same affective qualities as his later operas. They express human affect by defying in a similar fashion any simple iconicity. Mozart's genius was such that both his vocal and his nonvocal music conveys a scale of feelings that are infinitely encrusted with the ambiguities that belong to all affective attachments.

Only in masters like Mozart can we hope to find consummations of this sort. Schopenhauer thought that music reveals the will as it is in itself, as the ultimate force and basic energy that underlies everything in the world of appearance. He was thinking of purely abstract compositions, and he would probably have ranked them higher than music in a dramatic or operatic presentation. I believe he was mistaken in his approach to music, whether in opera or symphonic works. Through its expressiveness, music probes not a transcendental state of metaphysical being but rather the plenitude of sentiments and emotions that occur, often haphazardly, in mundane existence at every moment.

Produced by a lesser composer, music portrays affect in a pedestrian manner that teaches us little and provides only a meager consummation of our own desires. In the work of a Mozart the satisfaction we experience is not only greater and more permanent but also it shows how intricate and interwoven ordinary feelings must always be. In view of what our life in nature is, Schopenhauer's notion of the will explains almost nothing about this uncanny potency that music has.

We can discern as much by turning to Beethoven's one opera, *Fidelio*. In its beginning, which focuses upon the romantic plight of the jailkeeper's daughter, who is loved by one of her father's assistants but who prefers Leonore (disguised as a young man in her effort to free her husband Florestan), the drama is trivial and most of the music is relatively undistinguished. But when Beethoven presents the suffering of the political prisoners, the cruelty of Pizarro the warden, the heroism of Leonore as she risks her life to save Florestan from death, and her eventual success in overcoming tyranny by emancipating everyone who has been unjustly incarcerated—when all this happens in a crescendo of excitement mounting throughout the later scenes of this opera, we experience a consummation not only of musical expressiveness but also of moral, political, and religious idealizations that have resonated in millions of people for the last two hundred years.

Imperfect and chaotic as our active aspirations can be, we may not know how to renew in the outside world the enthusiasm stirred up by Beethoven's opera. It is so well constructed, so consummate within its musical fervor, that we may only leave the theater feeling wonderment before its grand originality and, if the production was any good, reverence for the performers who have brought it to us. But also we may experience a sense of having penetrated to something real and important in our affective fabric as human beings. Though the love between Leonore and Florestan is personal and marital, it enables them to struggle against evils inflicted upon mankind at large and not merely upon themselves. They are motivated by staunch self-interest that has merged with compassionate concern—in us as well as them—for anyone who suffers as the prisoners do.

In the nonmusical dramas from which Beethoven drew the plot of *Fidelio*, this appeal to our political and social sensibility did not, could not, evoke the affective response that his Singspiel elicits. The monumental issues require a harmonic enrichment that only music can provide. We need to hear the love, the hatred, the fury, the intensity of interpersonal confrontation through musical sounds over, or under, or within the action as they elaborate its implications. The feelings are communicated by means of technical and aesthetic wizardry that gives them their greatest magnification and expressiveness. Our affective attachments to others in our clan, our nation, our species, to our life, and possibly to life itself are then revitalized by these artistic consummations the composer has made available to us.

Human attachment is not just depicted or displayed in works like *Fidelio* and the *Ode to Joy* segment of Beethoven's Ninth Symphony. It is also created in the course of our aesthetic response to these masterful artifacts. That is why such music can have its strong effect upon our daily existence. *Fidelio* was performed at the reopening of the Vienna Opera House after World War II as a tribute to the human spirit that had been liberated after years of subjugation; and the Ninth Symphony served a similar function when Germany was unified as a democratic nation in 1989. Both works were meaningful on these occasions because of the feelings about humanity that were already incorporated in the music, itself a consummation of affective attitudes shared by many people. The music had this effect *through* its aesthetic quality, not because of something added onto it.

Some philosophers have argued that since only human beings, or other animals, have feelings it is mistaken to say that there can be affective consummation in music itself. But we do talk about musical passages being expressive even when they do not represent anything programmatically. This is an achievement in the art alone. Excellence in music is often determined by the affects it expresses, and *how* it expresses them.

By way of contrast to Mozart and Beethoven, consider the very popular musical *Les Miserables*, written by Claude-Michel Schönberg and Alain Boublil. The sentiments it expresses are reminiscent of the ones we find in Beethoven's music-drama. And yet we do not experience *Les Miserables* with the same sense of consummatory rightness in the relevant areas of affective attachment. Though its music is earnest, strongly rhythmic, and suitably emphatic in the choral singing on the battlements, its hypnotic melodies tend to be simplistic, overly repetitious, and minimally inventive.

The same might be said about gospel music and hymn-singing in church. But there the musical shortcomings are surmounted by the fact that the entire congregation can participate, however obliquely, in the vocal celebration of the oneness they all share through their communal faith. Perhaps Schönberg and Boublil were trying for that in a secular medium where the audience is expected to remain silent. This may have limited the consummatory possibilities of *Les Miserables*, while also accounting for whatever authenticity it does have.

❄

My comments about consummation as a motivating factor in art have mainly been accompanied by examples taken from the humanitarian or compassionate wing of the affective spectrum. Of equal importance is the ability of art to enliven, even satisfy, our sexual and romantic inclinations. I explore this and contiguous factors in *The Pursuit of Love*. My present discussion is designed to amplify those suggestions while serving as a passage to the aspect of affective attachments that I call "the aesthetic." In addressing that now, we might find that these remarks about artistic consummation may be extended to all other consummations in human experience. And if an extension of this sort is unrealistic, perhaps we can discover why.

4

The Aesthetic

In the welter of dualisms that have contributed to civilized mentality in the West, the distinction between the aesthetic and the rational has been among the most tenacious—above all, as this dichotomy generates the distinction between art and science. Though philistines and puritan fanatics in every age see little redeeming value in even the greatest artworks of their time, most societies have recognized, however grudgingly, the importance of aesthetic activities. Science is usually treated with more respect, as any key to magical power would be, but it too has often been considered dangerous and in need of governmental or ecclesiastic control.

From the very beginnings, philosophers sharply demarcated art and science as separate disciplines, much as the gods in the Platonic fable split the spherical hermaphrodites as a means of putting them in their place. In the modern world the recognized success of science has caused many practitioners of art criticism, art theory, and the arts themselves to imitate it whenever possible. On the other hand, scientific investigators who are aware of the recurrent limits to their pursuit of knowledge have often wondered whether art might not provide an alternate entry into the unknown. Some scientists have tried to add an alluring dignity to their reliance upon observation and theory construction by insisting that what they do in science is also artistic. A fully comprehensive account of how the values of art and science can be harmonized or interwoven has been harder to attain. We await the Leonardo who will lead the future in that direction.

The search for either scientific or aesthetic truth is relevant to the affective dimension of life as we are here exploring it. Both employ elements of imagination, idealization, and consummation. Even the imaginary, as I defined it, has a role in ordinary scientific methodology. When Einstein postulated that the universe is curved, he offered to the world of physics a metaphoric possibility that empirical research might then seek to validate through imaginative procedures congruent with technical ideals that demand their own completion. All scientists use idealizations as working hypotheses, and even as abstract models. They are based on nonverifiable hunches. Occasionally faith in the ultimate beauty or purposiveness of the cosmos is invoked as justification for some engaging theory. Einstein remarked that his general perspective was too beautiful not to be true and, in a specialized context, that God does not play dice with the universe. Latent within these not atypical responses is the scientist's belief that what seems right or consummatory to him or her as a professional will bring humankind that much closer to the final consummation of its yearning for what reason can recognize as total knowledge about everything that exists.

Given this similar deployment of imagination, idealization, and consummation, artistic and scientific interests might not seem to be unlike after all, or at least no more unlike than physics is from mathematics or music from painting. Perhaps our old, familiar taxonomies should be discarded entirely. But once we examine the nature of truth, or rather the different types of truth, we may find that art and science do indeed diverge. Without reinstating the unfortunate implications of the traditional dualism, we may conclude that the aesthetic has special and distinctive importance in affective attachments as a whole. Though sex, love, compassion, and the rest may be studied scientifically, as any psychological phenomena can be, the inner continuity that unites them to each other might belong directly to the aesthetic, and only indirectly to the scientific. This chapter tries to exploit that suggestion.

The word *aesthetic* is not old. It dates from German philosophy of the late eighteenth century. It originally referred to experience as it comes to us through our sense organs. In his *Critique of Pure Reason* Kant avails himself of this usage in order to express his ideas about the level of bare experience that must be categorized or interpreted before it can be perceived as arising from external reality. The "transcendental aesthetic" was needed to explain that without which there could be no consciousness that occurs in human beings. For Kant, the aesthetic was just the flood of sensations that impinge upon us, without form or meaning and yet essential for the meaningful structures that our mind imposes upon these incoming data. He thought our normal perception presupposes and includes the aesthetic, but also molds it into our conceptual awareness of objects whose organized patterns comprise what we take to be the world.

Kant employed this notion of the aesthetic in two related ways. First, it helped him formulate his belief that our quest for being-in-itself cannot be satisfied by reason alone, or more specifically by Reason that consists of a priori deduction rather than empirical observation. Though Reason purports to be a metaphysical faculty indigenous to the human mind, Kant argued, it can never disclose the ultimate nature of reality as contrasted with reality's appearance in human consciousness. All knowledge must therefore pertain to what is immediately present in experience. But that involves sensory awareness, which constitutes the aesthetic.

In tandem with this conception, Kant predicates another of equal importance. Just as Descartes asserted that the skeptic's act of doubting is itself indubitable, so too does Kant maintain that the presence of the aesthetic must be considered a *certainty* without which we could not understand the world as it exists. While the aesthetic cannot tell us what causes sensory data to be as they are, their constant occurrence is necessary and beyond any skeptical doubt. In providing mere sensation, the aesthetic serves as a prior condition for all possible experience.

In the two hundred years since Kant did his work, many philosophers have tried to refine these ideas about the "phenomenal" world delimited by sensations that in themselves can provide no knowledge of reality, that are just apparent qualities, and yet that possess their own type of certitude insofar as we can have no consciousness without them. This much of experience is immediate in being the nonderivative basis for whatever is given to our senses as one or another datum we just find at any moment of awareness.

I mention this development in the history of philosophy less for its relevance to epistemology or metaphysics than for its influence upon aesthetics. Having before them the Kantian doctrine about the aesthetic, a succession of philosophers applied his view to theories about the appreciation of art. What in colloquial language we now call "aesthetic" was assumed to be an intuition of life as it appears to experience in its bare immediacy. As opposed to any cognitive process, the immediate was identified with the sensations that underlie our varied perceptions of the world. These perceptions result from categories and concepts that we take for granted. But art, especially "fine" art, was thought to liberate us from our habitual mentality by regaling us with feelings and impressions as they are diversely presented by an artist within the formal limitations of his medium.

These ideas about art and its dependence on the aesthetic had different implications for different thinkers. For many Kantian philosophers the value art creates required analysis in terms of the same hedonic principles that apply to morals and the search for happiness. Others tried to locate aesthetic value in ideal possibilities of beauty that transcend the materiality emphasized by hedonist philosophy. Most of the Kantians believed that sensation, being directly given, was fundamental in art but still had to be supplemented by intellectual, even didactic, components. Otherwise, they insisted, art could not aspire to philosophic scope or general profundity. This approach was countered by those who claimed that artistic excellence depends entirely on the organizing of suitable data selected from sensory experience. Through its reliance on aesthetic form, art would thus attain its truthfulness to life.

We need not attempt to resolve these and the many other issues that confront philosophy of art in general. I wish to focus upon the suggestion that in the aesthetic we human beings may have access to something certain and immediate that helps create the world of our experience. Adequately explored, this notion may conceivably reveal the entire panoply of affective attachment. Though affect exceeds the boundaries of any one artistic medium, the affective character of our attachments may be related inwardly to the aesthetic element in all the arts. That is a possibility I will be studying in this place.

Feeling has its importance in arts such as music, film, literature, painting, and so on because, through their different techniques, they provide artificial but authentic fulfillments of affective needs. In its harmony with nature, spirit welcomes such contrived effects because they exemplify the consummate employment of imagination and idealization. In that capacity, the fine arts become the agencies of an aesthetic attitude native to themselves. Insofar as they plumb the depths of their origin in human reality, they can yield a treasured kind of "aesthetic truth." By determining what this is, we may be able to increase our understanding of affective attachment as well.

❊

In their attempt to analyze aesthetic truth, philosophers have occasionally begun by distinguishing between "truth about" and "truth to." Unlike the former, the latter is interpreted as suggesting that something is genuine or somehow congruent with the life we have known. Hearing an account that others dismiss as implausible, a person might reply that it seems true to his or her experience. It may also be said to "ring true," a phrase that comes from times when people could prove that a gold or silver coin was genuine by hitting it against a harder metal.

Utterances thought to have "truth to" are often called "nonpropositional" insofar as they do not say something that is overtly true or false, whereas an explicit assertion would have that capacity. The sentence "Unicorns once existed" is *about* unicorns; it states that they were real rather than just imagined entities. It claims to be true about them in a way that entails verifiability through observation of appropriate evidence. In distinguishing such truth from aesthetic truth, the philosophers in question maintain that works of art achieve their truthfulness not by conveying factual information about the world but rather by impressing us as insightful, though nonpropositional, presentations of human experience. This requires more than just felicity of form or beguiling materials. While it may also have realistic representational content, a work of art, even one that is highly conceptual or "philosophical," would get its aesthetic truth by being true to life without being propositional.

As an explanatory maneuver, this distinction between the two kinds of truth is faulty. I see the value in noting that some sentences are propositional and others not. But I find no reason to believe that the aesthetic truthfulness of art is inherently *non*propositional. Propositions may be expressed through suggestion and implication as well as through an explicit statement. If I ask you to close the window, I imply that it is now open. That belongs to the meaning of the words I use in my request. If I shudder as if I were cold while asking you to close the window, I am suggesting that more heat is needed in the room. Works of art, especially those that are fictive, may state little or nothing in the manner of an overt assertion. But through their reliance upon the imaginary, they are able to express truths about the world by virtue of implied and suggested propositions. That is what makes it possible for them to ring true in the sense of being genuine and deeply meaningful. The distinction between propositional and nonpropositional, between truth *about* and truth *to*, cannot do the work for which it was intended. Aesthetic truth includes each of the different sets of alternatives. It does so within a context that requires another mode of analysis.

There is one feature of the view that I am rejecting that nevertheless seems to me quite correct. In their ideas of truth, the philosophers I criticize do perceive a fundamental tie between artistic truth and the pervasive dimensions of experience common to all or many human beings. As a coin rings true so also does profundity in art fill our consciousness with an intuition (vague as it may be) that that's what life is like. We feel the rightness in what is being offered us regardless of how nonassertive and fictional it is. Through the work of art we have a sense of oneness with our reality; we feel that we are in touch and at-one with it.

Not all art can attain this kind of truthfulness, but great art does. It gives us a new entry into what is real by enlarging our awareness through imaginative extrapolations that may have previously exceeded our capacity.

The creativity of the artist makes this expansion possible. A work with aesthetic truth can include propositions that take the form of explicit assertion, as well as suggestion and implication, but it usually subordinates its assertive statements to those that are suggested or implied. This increases the play of imagination, and the imaginary in particular, allowing both to range through regions of our mentality which might have remained hidden in ordinary discourse. If the artifice or indirection deployed in this adventure of the spirit seems genuine, authentic to our condition, it is because we feel that we have reconnoitered something that is characteristic and significant in the life we all know. Aesthetic truth affects us as a renewable revelation of how things in general appear in human experience. It imparts what we call a "*sense* of reality." In the rest of this chapter I investigate the meaning of this concept.

❄

In saying that aesthetic truthfulness discloses what reality feels like to us, I am not suggesting that it uncovers a substratum of our consciousness. That would imply that it penetrates to a layer of our being that is more fundamental than the other levels. This image misled the philosophers who distinguished immediate experience from categories of interpretation that cover and hide it as one might clothe a naked body. The given was thought to reside beneath the cognitive machinery through which it finally shows itself completely processed by the intellect.

Analyses of this sort are not helpful. Whatever value they may have as epistemology they garner from something else in the original conception. That is the insight, which Kant clearly had in mind, that throughout our experience there occurs what he calls an "apperception" of experience. We have a consciousness that includes a sense of itself *as* consciousness. This much is undeniable, and it shows us how we can profitably use ideas of immediacy and the given. These do not signify a primal stratum in our being but rather the entire framework and comprehensive awareness of what we recognize as our experience at any time. The sense of this totality is vividly reawakened and represented by works of art that are true aesthetically. The ability to institute the reawakening and the representing of feelings of life as it exists in us is the key to aesthetic truth.

Since natural language is usually designed to serve the practical needs of happiness and survival, it is not well equipped to describe this phenomenon. Philosophers must therefore try, in their cumbersome way, to portray and reconstruct it. But though it is ever present within our sheer responsiveness as human beings, our awareness of what I am referring to may always remain obscure. I use this word in remembrance of Buñuel's film *That Obscure Object of Desire*. In it a man documents his obsession for a woman much younger than himself who keeps frustrating his sexual attachment to her and whose lifestyle he finds repellent. As much as he would like to exorcise himself, he cannot do so.

The entire movie is an inquiry, never accomplished, into the nature of his obscure objective, and what it is that he persistently desires without considering it desirable.

Though Buñuel's work deals with the special dilemmas of this interpersonal situation, all occasions of sexual attraction may be alike. Even when sex is consummated through hormonal excitement that culminates in a satisfying release of physical and psychological tension, we may feel that something has still escaped us. It is as if the reality of our powerful involvement lies beyond our grasp and adequate understanding. Delightfully wearied and relaxed, we can nevertheless wonder what the obscure object was that we craved so passionately at first but, even now that we have gained quiescence, remains unidentifiable.

One could reply that the object is obscure because it is buried in the archeological depths of reproductive instinct functioning in our species as in other primates, albeit for us occluded by accretions of intellect and civilized socialization. As Schopenhauer would say, the will—the energetic force in life—propels us into yearnings and related behavior that manifest only its monolithic urge to prolong the existence of life itself, regardless of anything else we care about. This is a metaphysical view, incapable of being verified. *It* is inherently obscure, by definition empirically unknowable. More evident in experience is the fact that human beings want to comprehend and express the sense of reality I mentioned earlier. That involves a diversity of feelings, evasive as they too may be, that everyone has just in being alive and conscious.

Allusions to a sense of reality often occur in everyday language. They arise in philosophical debate when further reasoning seems futile, as if the argument has reached a point where remaining disagreement can only indicate some ultimate difference of temperament or sensibility rather than intellect. Of course, there is more at stake than this. What we nominate as either temperament or as sensibility is itself the tip of an iceberg that floats through our past and present life like an affective island moving in the sea of our personal identity. To appreciate why philosophers perceive the world so differently, one would have to know how and why their contrasting feelings at a moment of final impasse represent the totality of their separate icebergs.

In meditating about this individual sense of reality that all men and women, not just philosophers, carry with them throughout their consciousness, we should resist the notion that each of us has a uniform membrane of awareness that encloses what we experience as our world and our response to it. The generalized sense of our existence as it uniquely pulsates within us will always have a variegated quality and changing configuration. Most people may even be oblivious of its actual presence. But in great art it becomes the pervasive aura of everything the artist creates, even if this creator does not conceptualize the meaning of what he or she has produced. Works of art achieve aesthetic truth by making an artist's sense of reality available to people, however different they may be, who can recognize and appreciate its unique authenticity.

I make these remarks in order to elucidate the ontological priority of the aesthetic in every mode of affective attachment. It is not only sexuality that entails an obscure desire but also interpersonal love, compassion, and forms of affect such as friendship, class solidarity, national pride, the love of humanity, or love of life itself. Within and throughout them all we seek a consummated oneness with whatever we sense as our reality. At its best, art reveals and instigates this attunement as the aesthetic truth some

medium is capable of achieving through its specialized
techniques. But the aesthetic is by no means limited to
(fine) art or the efforts of artists. The aesthetic impulse
exists in all interpersonal relations, in political and social
action, in scientific endeavor, in conscientious and devoted
behavior of every kind, and in play and the enjoyment of
benign idleness.

In the nineteenth century, especially among Romantic
thinkers of the time, the aesthetic was often ascribed to
earlier or more primitive stages of human development.
Childhood was idealized, and savages in a utopian past were
deemed noble, because of some innate access to aesthetic
response that civilization and technological maturity
presumably thwarts in the course of both phylogeny and
ontogeny. If they could approximate the mentality of
children and of primitives, adults in the West might
experience a type of happiness similar to theirs. So we are
told by Rousseau, Wordsworth, and others who ascribed the
failures of current existence to our acquired inability to live
in optimal rapport with the purely aesthetic.

This view was progressive insofar as it represented an
attempt to treat children and aborigines as human beings
with interests that were not to be submerged by the more
dominant attitudes of occidental grown-ups. Though
possibly sentimental and somewhat condescending, the
Romantics deflated the arrogance of Westerners who were
sure that the received values in their society are necessarily,
even metaphysically, superior to those of any other. All the
same, the new outlook was misguided. The aesthetic does
not fluctuate with different periods in life or levels of
civilization. We are engaged in our own sense of reality at all
times and under all conditions. The aesthetic can always be
enhanced by whatever circumventing goodness defines the
particularity of our individual experience. This vibrancy of

life will doubtless vary from person to person and from one age of maturity to another. But we all have equal access to the aesthetic as it exists for each of us in any circumstance.

There is no justifiable reason to idealize a single epoch in either individual or social development. As we get older, the aesthetic values of childhood may disintegrate or disappear; but they are followed by others that can be just as meaningful to us. In view of what we have become at the later date, they may or may not be more consummatory than those that were once accessible but no longer are. What matters most is how we use our everchanging aesthetic susceptibility. Being a child or a primitive cannot guarantee success in this regard, and being old and civilized is not necessarily an impediment. Since aesthetic consummations may exist for adults immersed in the workaday pursuits of modern life, they can give these people a sense of truthful oneness that is comparable to what is experienced by children, savages, or Romantic artists.

❄

My reflections about the nature of aesthetic truth may help us understand why human beings are often driven by a passionate need for justice, or knowledge, or lasting intimacy with a fellow creature. On the other hand, this line of thought can also explain why solitary contemplation or meditation has meant so much to so many people. If we can provide, however tentatively, some clarification about this bivalence, it might elucidate the role that affect plays throughout political and social affairs.

I begin with justice because it is the virtue that modern philosophers have considered foundational for ethical, hence commendable, attachments to other men and women. Once again, Kant's thought is a good point of departure. Having begun with the aesthetic as the epistemological grounding of all possible experience, Kant then turns away from it in his effort to explain the nature of morality. Since he believes that happiness results from consummatory completion of natural inclinations, Kant recognizes that aesthetic gratification has a place within the good life as a whole. But he claims that ethics, and justice above all, depends on principles of practical reason that systematically go beyond the aesthetic. His analysis is built upon the dualism he invokes to separate the two.

Kant and his followers insist upon this diremption between the aesthetic and the ethical because they believe that the former applies to subjective taste whereas the latter concerns itself with universal principles. What someone feels or immediately experiences issues from the aesthetic, according to Kant, and that may determine this person's love or lust or commiseration toward others. But what is right or wrong, ethically good or bad, just or unjust belongs to a different segment of human nature. Justice blinds itself to the feelings that occasion someone's personal concern or emotional affiliation. Justice hews to what is rational, rule-regulated, conceptually valid regardless of the pragmatic consequences.

Kant expounds similar ideas when he distinguishes between two kinds of love, each defining its own type of affective attachment: "Love out of inclination cannot be commanded, but kindness done from duty—although no inclination impels us, and even although natural and unconquerable disinclination stands in our way—is *practical* . . . , residing in the will and not in the propensions of feeling."[1] Kant wishes to analyze all of ethics, and specifically justice, in terms of rational mandates that may elicit appropriate sentiments, even a form of love, without being based upon a feeling of sympathy, compassion, or other personal inclination. In our generation this approach is represented by the work of John Rawls. Starting with the premise that people have their own self-oriented interests but must live together in a communal order, Rawls delineates the rational principles they can each accept as fair for everyone aside from anything they may individually feel or selfishly desire. Rawls presents this as an alternative to utilitarian beliefs that what is good or just is always a function of the greatest happiness for the greatest number of human beings.[2]

Within utilitarianism itself, including the version of John Stuart Mill, there is a similar assumption that neither compassion nor any other affect—however exemplary it may be—can account for the rules that determine the nature of justice. They must be formulated in terms of general utility. Both this and the Kantian way of thinking about ethics were contested by Schopenhauer and, before him, by Shaftesbury, Hutcheson, and other adherents to what is called "moral sentiment theory." More recently, Robert C. Solomon has continued their critique by asserting related ideas in the context of his belief that reason and emotion cannot be separated as Kant or even Mill envisaged.[3]

If, however, we reject this dualism that has become the mainstream of post-Kantian Western philosophy, we must still show how—on some occasions at least—ethical principles can justifiably constrain our affective inclinations, our search for happiness, and even our preferences in sex or love. If it is not sufficient to say that justice entails rational rules that manifest a need for a priori control over self-oriented desires, we must find some other way of explaining why we do accept the legitimacy of moral impositions upon our feelings and behavior. I suggest that the basis, the inner sanction, of this acceptance must reside in our inability to detach our aesthetic sense of reality from our concern for other living creatures as fellow participants in nature.

❄

This statement is highly compressed and has to be unpacked. I will try to do so step by step. Some philosophers would claim that justice, or morality in any form, can have no meaning except in conditions that involve other persons. Is it unjust, they say, for us to eat animals we have raised for that purpose, to kill insects that interfere with our comfort, to uproot species of every kind that impede our use of planet Earth? Even to build a highway, we must dislodge millions of ants that would never have been a threat to our well-being. Is there any injustice or immorality in our destroying them? Like most human beings, we may agree that there is not. But we would feel differently about torturing insects for reasons that are sadistic or merely willful. We would say that such conduct is wrong.

Without stretching normal conceptions of morality very far, we might well feel it is unjust to wreak unnecessary and unmerited harm upon any creature whatsoever. Whether or not we believe that animals have rights—and if they do, why not insects and all other kinds of life?—we can easily pose questions of justice far beyond human relations alone.

This fluidity in our thinking about justice results from the fact that we identify with many animals: we realize that we are animals ourselves. We also identify with various other living creatures. We see our similarity in many respects; we intuit a kinship—normally unadmitted or ignored—with virtually any manifestation of vitality. If our ideas of justice or ethics are indeed applicable to other species, though it is sometimes very hard to know which ones to include in such reasoning, our identifying with them must have great relevance in whatever morality we are likely to espouse. I suggest that identification of this sort creates affective attachments without which neither justice nor ethics could exist as they do in human experience.

✻

As an illustration of this dimension in our feelings, consider the overlap between ethics and metaphysics which structures common beliefs about "the sanctity of life." Many people are strongly convinced that the taking of innocent human life is evil. The word *innocent* is crucial here because those who consider murder to be the greatest of crimes are often willing to condone the execution of persons who commit murders. Killing another in self-defense is likewise acceptable to virtually everyone; and the fact that members of nonhuman species must lose their lives in order for us to feed on them has been disturbing only to a small number of vegetarians. The notion of life as sacred is therefore an indefinite, but quasi-religious, feeling that tints our consciousness, though variably from one individual to another.

Even those who oppose abortion, or euthanasia, or outright suicide, rarely try to defend their views on utilitarian grounds; and abstract philosophical concepts such as Kant's categorical imperative may not enter into their deliberations at all. Whatever people think about the killing of animate creatures, they base their convictions about the sanctity of life on heartfelt sentiments that are too deep and too broad to depend upon much rational inspection.

In these metaphysico-moral issues, other affirmations also play a part. Opponents of abortion will claim that the fetus, which is indubitably human in some sense of that word and whether or not this bit of life can be called a person, must enjoy the same rights as children or adults.

People who consider euthanasia immoral may deny that anyone is entitled to shorten another person's life even as an act of mercy. Some thinkers have argued that suicide is a kind of murder perpetrated upon oneself. In the history of philosophical reflection about such matters, debate has rarely ventured beyond assertions or denials equivalent to these. Little has been said about the more fundamental sentiment that I am trying to elucidate—the somewhat mystical feeling that life is sacred in ways that have immediate significance for the making of practical decisions about how we should live and die.

Can we get any helpful clarification about these delicate and, one might say, shapeless views about mere existence? Our difficulties are compounded by the fact that this type of awareness and concern generally occurs in a highly nebulous form. As always, I find that I can proceed only by delving into an experience of my own. When I was a teenager, a draft of one of Mark Twain's novels had a great effect on me. The novel is *The Mysterious Stranger*, and editors have given the draft the same title although it is actually a separate novella. In this draft Twain constructs a fable about a visit to earth by an alien being, as our science fiction nowadays would probably call him. He is an angel who comes from a prominent family in heaven, and he is endowed with the miraculous powers that all angels have. Though his name is Satan, like his renowned relative who rebelled and had to be punished, there is no suggestion that he is in fact a devil or an outcast. Nevertheless he has a disdainful and even cruel attitude toward members of our species. This perturbs the young fellows whom he befriends, and it makes them wonder whether he is basically evil rather than good.

As a divertissement for the boys, Satan creates a colony of miniature men and women whose petty foibles he and they observe with great amusement. But when the constant squabbling among these creatures becomes tiresome, Satan simply crushes them. He has no feeling for the life he has extinguished in so casual and peremptory a manner. The boys are appalled. They cannot distinguish what he has done from wanton and malicious murder.

Satan, who reads their thoughts, replies that the slaughtered humanoids "were of no value. . . . We can make plenty more."[4] He had previously told his new friends that he and all the other angels "cannot do wrong; neither have we any disposition to do it, for we do not know what it is."[5] Even so, the idea that life, not just the life of animated figurines but life as a whole—and the life of human beings in particular—should be an expendable commodity continues to trouble the boys.

Their distress increases throughout the novel as Satan points out the inferiority of what Twain calls in another book "the damned human race." While his young pupils are convinced that Satan is a wonder-working psychopath, the angel teaches them that the cause of human misery and degradation is precisely that moral sense by which they seek to judge him. Far from being one of the higher animals, man is dragged down by his conception of morality: "When a brute inflicts pain he does it innocently; it is not wrong; for him there is no such thing as wrong. And he does not inflict pain for the pleasure of inflicting it—only man does that. . . . He [man] is always choosing, and in nine cases out of ten, he prefers the wrong."[6]

Having proved that human existence has virtually no value, Satan can finally reconcile the boys to his shortening the lives of people who are destined for heaven after death. The chosen ones are thereby spared any pointless suffering on earth while being accorded a longer sojourn in the better place beyond. A similar notion appears in several plays of

Shakespeare. But he usually presents this reasoning as duplicity used by villains who commit murder for selfish purposes. In *The Mysterious Stranger* the idea serves to reinforce Satan's superior belief about the relative worthlessness of our life and its lack of any sanctity.

I myself have always shared the horror felt by the boys. Reading the novel for the first time, I distrusted Satan's credentials and expected that Twain's dénouement would show him to be a fraud, a celestial criminal of one type or another. I have always recoiled from the spectacle of Napoleon surveying the dead French soldiers at Austerlitz and saying to his generals that a good night in Paris will remedy these losses—as if it was only a matter of planting more seeds.

In the Bible we learn that the patience and unshakable submissiveness of Job are eventually rewarded by his getting a new set of children as compensation for those that God had killed in testing Job's religious faith. As a youngster I was puzzled by the suggestion that human lives were replaceable in this fashion. Were all the earlier sons and daughters just a herd of cattle whose lives did not count for anything in themselves? We are not told that Job's paternal joy in his later children was tempered, even slightly, by his grief for the ones he had lost. This official callousness strengthened my conviction that much of Western religion is predicated upon an insensitivity, indeed irreverence, toward life. Yet people who do insist upon the sanctity of life are often devout Jews, Christians, Moslems. How can this paradox be resolved? And if one professes no religious faith, how can one hold that life is at all sacred?

I believe that the only way out is to recognize how often human beings sense a oneness with other life, above all if it is life that resembles and intersects their own without threatening it. This is an aptitude we have *as* human beings, which is to say, as creatures aware of their origin in nature. It requires no extranatural explanation.

In *The Harmony of Nature and Spirit* I described the feeling of identification with others in its relation to empathy. I argued that compassion, as an offshoot of empathy, is foundational in ethics. Our sense of justice preeminently devolves from these and related dispositions—for instance, militant enthusiasm in defense of a humanitarian cause, or revulsion and anger toward those who harm people out of unmitigated selfishness, or indignation, hatred, vengeful emotion toward someone who infringes upon our rights. These feelings are not mere *consequences* of our recognition that a system of fairness or innate rationality has been violated. They are instead basic responses without which justice and morality could not exist.

Whether affirmative or negative, the underlying sentiments generate standards of behavior that *become* ethically meaningful to us. Sympathy and compassion are positive reactions to the hardship of others, sympathy as a way of duplicating and displaying the affective tone of their suffering, compassion as the doing of what must be done to alleviate and remove it. Anger, hatred, and the craving for revenge vent our fury at seeing life trampled, either in our own person or in someone else's. As the context of action and decision making, moral sentiments arise from deep within our reality as human beings. They express our sense of what it is to be animate as we and all other creatures are, organically motivated and therefore more than just a bit of matter that can be used at will. Like everything else that lives, we are made of matter; but, like all the rest, we share a vital spark that makes us something more as well.

Rationality has great importance in its ability to formulate and present the implications of moral affect. We employ reason to codify standards that regulate our feelings, that transmute them into habits beneficial in life and readily inculcated as guides for difficult choices. Though these choices are geared to pertinent feelings, whether spontaneous or nurtured, they require a conceptual structure that is both interpersonal and relatively uniform. Otherwise they would not be meaningful for everyone who is involved.

Language is the medium for this social innovation. It creates a kind of communal objectivity. In themselves the feelings, the emotions, the inclinations that comprise our affective attachments are too diffuse and too ephemeral for the purposive needs of ethics or of justice. The moral sentiments are better conveyed in an art form like poetry or drama or operatic music, each of which may even provide a representation of what happens in an imaginary law court. But too much attention to feeling would be disruptive in a real one.

Rationality is admirably suited to handle this problem. It introduces methods of inductive and deductive logic into the adjudication of human dilemmas. It makes possible casuistry that affect alone could never yield. Moreover, it engenders persuasive sentiments of guilt and shame as well as the type of conscience that incorporates them. All this presupposes a system of integrated rules that practical reason invents for the sake of inducing general acquiescence.

What reason *cannot* supply is the affective integument out of which justice or morality comes into being. That requires the nonrational determinants that constitute what is present to us as the felt apprehension of our innermost reality, our sense of ourselves as social creatures immersed in the aesthetic immediacy we constantly experience. This encloses even rationality within itself. What distinguishes ethics and justice from any other manifestation of the aesthetic is their ability to prescribe the character of authorized conduct. They do so by drawing upon feelings that sustain their imperious mandates. Without those feelings, they ossify and become rigid formulae: they degenerate into empty legalisms and meaningless virtues.

When we act morally, or when justice has been upheld, we experience an aesthetic rightness in ourselves. It is a feeling like the one we have in relishing the truthfulness of a great work of art. In the ethical situation we feel: "That's how all of life *ought to be, and may become!*". In the artistic: "That's how life *appears to one who is able to experience it as it is!*". The verbs in these utterances are left unanalyzed because they signify imaginative possibilities so vast that only our sense of reality can entertain them. Some works of art combine the different types of feeling by employing morality or justice as a constitutive theme within their creative harmony—for instance, in the last scene of *Fidelio*, or in any comedy where the good people win out and the wicked are finally punished. The aesthetic truth in these ethical resolutions reattaches us to what we think that human existence is potentially and should be like in actuality.

❋

I call this a *re*attachment because its effect is felt most forcefully only after we have lost our preanalytic faith in a benign and comforting oneness that binds us to the world. Intellect causes that loss as an unintended result of its attempt to keep us alive at any cost. The sense of being a separate self emerges from myriad experiences we undergo in seeking to survive. They can lead us to enjoy, and bestow value upon, the freedom and autonomy of our separateness. But they can also induce sentiments of alienation or despair. In the next chapter I return to that consequence of having forfeited the feeling that we are at-one with nature.

Kant's solution is worth discussing here. In the first phase of his mature philosophy, Kant repudiates the metaphysical credibility of pure Reason in the context of his affirmation about the epistemological ultimacy of the aesthetic. So radical is his critique, however, that it sweeps away all traditional belief in a transcendental soul, a God who exists eternally outside time and space, and almost every moral and religious dogma that belonged to Judeo-Christian orthodoxy. Being an honest and unrelenting philosopher, Kant was willing to push the argument wherever it could go. But as a human being in the everyday reality that required him to exercise his will and make ethical decisions, he felt stymied by the conclusions to which his reasoning had led him. He saw the good life as one that includes both happiness and the realization that we are acting morally, which is to say, in accordance with our conscience. But these two conditions cannot be met, he thought, unless one believes that the virtuous will indeed be rewarded and the wicked punished. Since the opposite often happens in the world as we know it, Kant predicated a life after death in which ethical merit is recompensed by well-earned happiness. That would vindicate our sense of justice.

Having taken this mammoth step, Kant proceeds to reinstate many of the traditional doctrines of Western religion. When he asks himself why he has to take the step at all, he admits that rationality alone cannot justify it. He recognizes that he has made an act of faith, an expression of feelings that he has chosen to accommodate instead of throttling for whatever reason. By way of explanation, all he can say is that life would be unbearable for him unless he believed the tenets he is now willing to affirm. So powerful is his need to exist as a conscientious and possibly righteous person, as a moral agent who gives the utmost importance to being ethical, to being free of painful guilt, that he *must* accept whatever ideas enable him to live that way. He knows his response is personal or subjective, and only defensible as such. But he feels he cannot go on without it. In other words, his declaration is an affective gesture that reattaches him to what he takes to be the sense of his reality.

In making this dramatic closure to his philosophy, Kant reverts to his views about the aesthetic. As it is primary in the acquisition of knowledge, so too does it show what is necessary for there to be a unified and consummatory sense of reality. As awareness that the aesthetic is qualitatively immediate in experience gives insight into the empirical world our intellect then constructs, so too does our feeling of what seems aesthetically right to us as moral beings establish an ultimate meaning in our lives.

From these Kantian ideas about aesthetic elements within our sense of reality, Kierkegaard evolved his conception of religious faith. For him it is an absurdist act that enables us to rebuild our broken humanity beyond the capacity of reason. The Kantian approach also leads to William James's notion of a will to believe under conditions where arguments for and against religion are balanced or inconclusive.

Of equal interest is the manner in which Kant combines the thinking of Hume and Luther at this juncture. Hume could give no justification for our conventional belief in causality or the existence of the external world other than the fact that neither he nor anyone else can live without these unreasoned assumptions. Hume says that when he joins the company of other people, he must put his analyses aside as socially and practically irrelevant to the mundane world in which he normally exists. He understands that he is responding in an affective, aesthetic, and mainly subjective way, but he cannot imagine any other possibility if life is to continue. It would be like refusing to breathe the air once we learn that it is made up of molecules. We have to accept on faith the epistemological principles that skeptical reason undermines, just as we have to inhale oxygen regardless of what we know about its chemistry.

Luther's defense of his Christian faith is similar. He insists that reason can always find doubts in whatever our religious feelings lead us to accept, and yet the great urgency of those feelings must take precedence. I think that is part of what Luther may have meant when he proclaimed, at the Diet of Worms: "I can do no other. Here I stand."

❋

This act of faith, this affective self-affirmation in resolving the cosmic issues that religion and philosophy address, may be sufficient for great thinkers like Kant, Hume, and Luther, or for saints and mystics who are inspired by some other message. These are all extraordinary people, living (and suffering) at a height most human beings could not reach even if they wanted to. For the large majority of us, the aesthetic attachment I am discussing must occur in a different setting. Though our sense of justice, and our concept of justice itself, is based on feelings of compassion or resentment catalogued and transmuted by the formalistic reasoning of others, our immediate concern about such matters includes something more. Whether the response is belief about right and wrong or a feeling about what is fundamental in our sense of reality, it comes through the mediation of individuals we have taken as authorities.

In childhood these authorities are usually the mother and the father, combined as an ostensive symbol of everything that matters, everything the child wants to feel oneness with. But mothers and fathers often disagree among themselves, quarrel and even vitiate each other's credibility. Sometimes that may reinforce the child's healthy need to break away from both and find a separate destiny. But in doing so and in growing up to be an adult, the child encounters other authorities, some of whom may be better than its parents in evoking affirmative attitudes that make one feel at home in the universe and in the realm of values.

The new authority figures are charismatic men and women of whatever stripe who embody the luminosity of living reality and the splendor of self-assurance about moral or aesthetic possibilities. We miss the point if we assume that the emotive outburst of a teenager swooning before a famous rock star can be reduced to mere libidinal excitement. Sex is undoubtedly a part of what is happening, but more important is the fact that the teenager has invested in the hypnotic personality the capacity to represent the emblazoned image of all that is real and good. One might call this love, but it is not interpersonal as in romantic love. Neither is it a form of compassion, even of the indirect type that explains the nature of justice. It is instead an expression of feeling that amalgamates the impetus of sex, the playfulness of imagination evoked by arts such as music, and the momentary certainty of being close to reality and the quality of life. All this makes us feel united with the world in which we live. If that world is a sizable group of screaming enthusiasts more or less like oneself, the affective charge can be irresistible.

I mention rock stars as the modern vortex of this attachment because they perform their godlike calling throughout the world, and especially in the most advanced countries. At the same time they have less directive power, though they may get greater financial rewards, than the political and so-called spiritual leaders in most societies. A prime, but by no means unique, example in our age is the adulation of Chairman Mao that mesmerized a nation of almost a billion people during the Cultural Revolution in China. In previous periods the emperor had been considered godlike and was treated as a divine spokesman in matters of religion as well as public policy. But never before had the celestial personality been able to arouse as much intense emotion as Chairman Mao. Having unified China after World War II, he was the father of his country as it then existed. But also Mao introduced detailed prescriptions that affected daily life, disseminating rules of conduct and conformity through the little red book. He remained in undisputed power for many more years than his young devotees could remember.

Being an atheist in an atheistic world of his own creation, Mao did not have to represent divinity. He could radiate it from within himself. He had a kind of religious and ethical charisma that no pope or institutional envoy of God can hope to emulate. In organizing the fervor of Chinese boys and girls, the Cultural Revolution had its immense effect because Mao, or rather his image, served not only as a creative father but also as a protective mother and a Christlike savior of the nation. Moreover, he was revered as an original thinker, even poet, of the first rank. No ordinary politician, artist, or philosopher could possibly elicit the strong emotions that surged throughout the affective attachment of his followers.

Charismatic leaders have their control over us because of our awed respect for their success in coping with realities that we cannot understand or manipulate. They create faith in their political as well as ethical superiority and unassailable wisdom. We have a need for such people because we cherish the ecstatic feeling that *through* the charismatic leader we too can touch reality. These sentiments are metaphysical, as they are in the consummatory experience afforded by a profound and moving work of art. As a historical event, the Cultural Revolution was, in fact, a venture in living theater involving participation by a cast of millions. It was an aesthetic artifact, a continuous soap opera expressing moral, social, and quasi-religious feeling.

Though their ideology was conservative rather than radical, the Greek tragedies must have been similar to the Cultural Revolution, especially when they were followed by a satyr play that promised general happiness as the upshot of all the suffering enacted in the previous segments. Being an offshoot of polytheistic religion, ancient tragedy had numinous heroes who differed from those that autocracy or monotheism make eminent in our modern imagination. But the affective attachments must surely have been alike.

❋

In the foreword to a recent book that tries to merge Buddhist teachings with Western modes of psychotherapy, the Dalai Lama asserts that "The purpose of life is to be happy." He then claims that his religion affords the "inner peace" and "calming" of the mind that makes it possible to attain this goal.[7] Needless to say, the Dalai Lama is not referring to hedonistic ideas about happiness or consummation that have been prevalent and exhaustively developed in Western culture. He obviously identifies "true" happiness with the peaceful and calming states created by Buddhist techniques. But whence arise the affective benefits that may result from such practices, as they exist either in themselves or in conjunction with psychiatric therapies that have been more common in the West?

The conglomeration of Buddhist methods designed to yield the happiness of spiritual freedom is called "meditation."

What has generally gone by the name of "contemplation" is its counterpart in Western religion and philosophy. The two are systematically different, however, since they originate from different beliefs about the nature of being. Where the contemplative attitude, particularly in Christianity, presupposes the distinction between appearance and reality inherited from Plato, meditation tends to avoid any such idea even though some forms of Buddhist faith retain dualistic elements derived from the Hinduism out of which they grew.

Contemplation may be directed toward cognitive apprehension of abstract entities, as in Plato's doctrine of forms and Santayana's conception of "essences." In traditional Christianity contemplation belongs to a search for loving union with divinity, as portrayed by Saint Augustine or Saint Bernard. It is most often depicted as an effort that an individual self makes in order to elevate but also cleanse itself through oneness with the reality intuited as metaphysically ultimate. The meditative approach has another orientation. It is offered as a way of eliminating the concept of self entirely. It emphasizes "bare attention" or inward insight as devices for discovering, and also eradicating, the causes of human distress through detached awareness of what they are. No transcendental dogmas are asserted.

These two paths of salvation are the same in one respect that is rarely understood by devotees of either. Though Christian contemplation pursues eternal bliss attainable after death while Buddhist meditation seeks nirvana, interpreted as either heaven or pure nothingness, both try to instill a capacity for serenity in life that is supremely satisfying, whatever else it may be. Each promises a kind of total happiness that only religion can bring about. But what does this entail?

I do not think we can find a univocal answer to that question. Mystics of either persuasion, believers in either approach, give reports about their experience that suggest a great variety in the promised happiness or fulfillment. The goal is sometimes described as conceptual enlightenment or awakening, sometimes as emotional gratification, sometimes as joy or boundless ecstasy, sometimes as contentment, sometimes as dissolution of earthly travails, sometimes as transformation of sorrows into harmonious resignation. What unites these and related states is the fact that imagination combined with one or another form of idealization has induced a consummatory outcome that is aesthetic, rather than merely intellectual or practical.

Part of the process that these spiritual disciplines have in common requires a concentration upon troubled or undesirable aspects of oneself that are worked through in one manner or another and then conquered by internal forces hitherto unused. Something comparable happens in the experience of great art. It grips our attention by arousing conflicting responses that are specially selected because they express difficulties we must confront in life. The work of art introduces tension for the sake of bringing it to a satisfying, though possibly sad or tragic, conclusion. This resolution within the artificial parameters of an artistic medium can thus effect a catharsis, as Aristotle called it. Under these controlled conditions the purgation of feeling may strengthen our ability to cope with urgent but possibly unmanageable problems in the real world.

Contemplation and meditation, or some cognate of theirs, also resemble art in aiming for the affective response I have been describing as an experience of aesthetic truthfulness arising from a person's sense of reality. Far from being detached or taken out of the world, we are reattached more securely to that much of nature that lends itself to the consummations available through the widest reach of our creative imagination.

As many scholars have noted, the modes of spirituality developed in both Eastern and Western religions are subject to alternate interpretations by their own adherents. I mentioned one difference of opinion when I suggested that nirvana can be thought of as a heavenly abode or else as absolute nothingness. I leave this problem to experts in the field. What interests me most is the fact that when the various views are presented as viable methods for attaining a good life in nature as we understand it, and by reference to the values we recognize as meaningful for most people, the types of life enhancement they promise are often very much alike. They resemble each other in announcing the possibility of an all-inclusive sense of rightness, one that permanently dissolves the anxieties and many of the doubts that characterize our existence. Despite their programmatic and theoretical disparity, they offer similar consummations that bloom within their own kind of aesthetico-religious experience.

If we begin with this approach, attempts to reconcile post-Freudian psychoanalysis with Buddhist or Christian or other theological teachings may well succeed. But even within the naturalism of psychoanalytic theory, many doctrines associated with it are justifiable only as a means of promoting aesthetic values that are instrumental to living a good and happy life.

In the development of Freud's ideas, this becomes apparent at several points. For instance, he dedicates his professional career to the study of instincts as the basis of a purely scientific theory about the nature of motivation. But at the end of his life he admits that "Instincts are mythical entities, magnificent in their indefiniteness. In our work we cannot for a moment disregard them, yet we are never sure that we are seeing them clearly."[8] Making such remarks, Freud attests not only to the magnificence of the mythic despite its indefiniteness but also to the importance of recognizing this anomalous and scarcely objective equilibration in our thought. If one does *that*, however, one acknowledges how thoroughly the aesthetic permeates even quasi-scientific speculations in psychology.

At other times Freud confesses, as some of his followers have, that the therapy he advocates can do little more than help a patient to quiet anxieties by accepting the fact that discomforts are unavoidable in human nature. In one place he calls normality "an ideal fiction."[9] To some extent at least, he means that our usual idea of what is normal includes various goals that imagination has concocted as perfections we can only envisage as mere possibilities. Though the cognitive status of normality is thereby brought into question, Freud treats this fictional construction as a comprehensive guide in our pursuit of a life worth living. He perceives that, fictive as they may be, ideals are able to assuage the conflict within an ego whose abnormality is, as Freud says, "unfortunately no fiction."

This can happen, I suggest, only in the context of an affective adjustment that seems right to us because it makes us feel at-one with ourselves as just the human beings that we think we are. When that occurs, we have an aesthetic experience that is attuned to our sense of reality. Attachments that issue from this product of the idealizing imagination will be consummatory in some degree.

❄

For another example of the aesthetic in relation to affective attachment, we can now turn to Nietzsche's concept of *amor fati*. This is the idea that a capacity for cosmic love, through which we love everything indiscriminately, conduces to "greatness in a human being."[10] In previous discussions of the notion, I have moved progressively closer to it, but without being able to agree. In the hope of making Nietzsche's view more plausible, I reinterpreted it as meaning that all things, however hostile or evil, may be treated as a priori candidates for our love whether or not we can actually love them as they are. But even in saying this, I felt that Nietzsche intended something else—a loving attitude toward everything imaginable, bad or foul as it may be. That seemed to me like an inauthentic love, and even an absurdity, if only because most of the universe is beyond our acquaintance or comprehension.

In that regard, my thinking has not much changed. On the other hand, the deliberation in this chapter brings me to an additional thought about Nietzsche's concept. Amor fati can be seen in the context of other revolutionary ideas that Nietzsche developed piecemeal throughout the two decades of his creative life. He left many of these suggestions in the fragmentary notes that were collected after his death in the book entitled *The Will to Power* that philosophical naturalists have recently attempted to carry forward. These final speculations are related to Nietzsche's attack upon the distinction between appearance and reality. If the notion of amor fati makes sense, it can possibly do so as a consequence of our belief that all things in the world have their own indefeasibility as irreducible particulars whose being must not be subordinated or rendered inferior to the greater reality of some transcendental realm beyond the one we encounter in experience.

During his last period, Nietzsche also introduces the definition of love as a "spiritualizing of sensuality."[11] He uses this phrase in *The Twilight of the Idols*, which he wrote shortly before the mental and physical collapse that ended his intellectual development. His remarks are tantalizing, since he never clarifies what he means by the word *spiritualizing*. Does it refer to a Hegelian category of mind? Is it something that directs itself toward Being that underlies the Becoming of nature, as many idealists (including Hegel, in the usual interpretation) would have claimed? How is "sensuality" capable of being spiritualized? And what would be an example of this harmonization between apparent opposites?

Nietzsche makes virtually no attempt to answer questions such as these. But in his terminal remarks about the will to power he shows where he was heading. His comments clearly indicate that the power he advocates, the greatness in a human being to which he alludes, results from the creativity of art. The artist manifests the ideal of the superman. And since life as a whole must be perceived as having the ability to become an art form in itself, the goals of ethics and religion can be attained only through the consummation of our most extensive and creative longings. For that to happen, we must accept and even welcome everything that exists, and all possible experience, as material for a supreme work of art. Presumably that would be the consummation of our entire life, lived in its immediacy and as an aesthetic achievement. Therein lies the meaning of spiritualization, not only of sensuality but also of everything else that belongs to our humanity.

This interpretation of what Nietzsche might have been groping for under the rubric of amor fati may or may not be correct as exegesis. In either event, we can still wonder whether the concept of universal love has been rendered more convincing. Must spiritualization of the senses be taken to imply that the good life, and the life of spirit itself, requires an ability to love everything *indiscriminately*? In my judgment that difficulty has not been resolved.

Nor is faith in amor fati buttressed by the (Nietzschean) belief that the aesthetic accounts for the goodness of affective attachments in general. Those who feel cosmic love will have an experience of the world which is not the same as for those who do not have cosmic love. Yet neither alternative is necessarily preferable. As with all diversity in religious or metaphysical orientation, people bestow value upon whatever seizes them as coherent with their own sense of reality. We have no reason to doubt that their different feelings of oneness may be equally or equivalently consummatory. Maintaining our pluralistic outlook, we can freely admit that the conflicting attitudes can proffer satisfying attachments distinctive to themselves. We may even credit them with having grasped their own form of aesthetic truth. But no attachment like the one that Nietzsche recommends can have preeminence over every other. Each depends upon the individual ideals and consummations created by a person's imagination. Each justifies itself by being conducive to someone's ability to live a meaningful and happy life as he or she perceives it. This need not include anything like the amor fati Nietzsche had in mind.

5

Affective Failure
and Renewal

In his writings Nietzsche occasionally expresses concern about the possible consequence of his work. He feared that others might not be able to benefit from it. He worried about the effect upon the world of his atheism, his tragic view of life, his glorification of power, his adoration of the artist. Assuming that his thought prevails in a hundred years, he asked, would the future nihilists go mad, despair of all religions and systems of value, commit suicide perhaps rather than face the cosmic loneliness of being human? He himself inherited the grim outlook of his Lutheran parents, against whom he could profitably rebel. But that type of adaptation would no longer be available for those in the twentieth or twenty-first century whose forebears had already been awakened by his philosophy to the nothingness of life. What would happen to these latter-day Nietzscheans?

We now know that many people in our disenchanted centuries have reverted to the older creeds, sometimes with extremism and bigotry that would have disgusted Nietzsche. Regardless of such frightening consequences, the human need for meaning can be satisfied by reactionary attitudes as well as by enlightened awareness. What we may learn from Nietzsche's problem is therefore something that lies beneath the surface of anything he says explicitly. In asking whether future generations can cope with the harsh truths about their condition as he interprets it, Nietzsche is delving into our ability to confront and surmount the defeat of dreams, of longings, of idealistic aspirations that have so greatly mattered to almost everyone.

No discussion about attachments can be honest or acceptable without the realization that affective bonding rarely succeeds as we would like it to. While advocating yea-saying and love for even an evil cosmos, Nietzsche's optimistic message is always a reverberating response to the Schopenhauerian pessimism from which it can never free itself entirely. Deep down Nietzsche would seem to agree with Schopenhauer that nature evokes our desire for attachment of many sorts but secretly contrives to thwart most, and possibly all, of them.

I feel the tension within this naturalistic quandary. We can understand the positive character of affective attachments only by explaining their frequent failure, and why they fail as often as they do. Since human nature has no single, essential, structure or all-pervading impulsion toward some goal that is sanctioned by objective reality, it is always divided within itself. We are a complexity of variable forces, of changing tropes competing with each other for dominance at every moment and throughout all circumstances. These circumstances are themselves in perennial flux. Our failures result from alterations in the environment as well as in our own evolving predilections. Success in life is paid for by diminution in the values we may have once sought but do not any more.

❊

Trying to clarify the dialectic between failure and success in relation to affective attachment, I begin with a distinction among three types of failure. Though the terminology I use may be a little stipulative, the reader will easily recognize the differences between "alienation," "estrangement," and "detachment," as I shall call them. Each pertains to its own kind of affect, and all are able to eventuate in successes that might never have occurred without them.

Through alienation we suffer the results of being cut off from some power or mode of existence that we ourselves accept as an ideality we care about. Sinners feel alienated from God because they believe that their waywardness prevents them from sharing in the infinite goodness the deity is willing to afford. Criminals or disenfranchised people feel alienated from the state because they know it systematically denies them rights and privileges for which they hunger. If the alienated condition has been caused for reasons that are unjust, that may occasion a further level of alienation. It will mean that another system of what one values has been withdrawn.

Alienation has long been seen as a serious problem for our culture at its present stage of technological development. I discuss this in my book on the art of film. I argue that the automatic technology of the camera creates a sense of alienation that may be indigenous to all cinematic efforts. At the same time, I claim that film is the most exciting art form of our time because it succeeds so greatly in overcoming the alienation it itself creates as if to exemplify humanity's constant struggle with alienation from material nature.[1]

This failure and success through alienation is not caused by technology as such. I never feel alienated from my spoon or fork, which are simple types of technology, when I use them in the eating of a meal. They are, for me, just passive instrumentalities. Whether or not they perform their function well, they rarely impinge upon my desire to feel attached to the edible world I appropriate with their help. Neither do I feel alienated from my computer, even when it breaks down or resists my desire to master it. I normally experience the computer as a faithful servant whose rapid responsiveness encourages me to seek attachments to other people (to you, the reader, for instance) and to remote aspects of my own being as an author.

The camera differs from personal computers and from household utensils inasmuch as it is a technology that produces automatically, though directed by human beings that give it general commands. The automation creates a concatenation of meanings through its omnipresent operation within this art form. It itself is part of the process of transforming reality which characterizes the cinematic medium. Whether or not the camera tries to record or duplicate reality, its automatic technology creates visual and sonic means of communicating feelings and ideas about the world it discloses. While alienating us from immediate contact with the objects or persons that interest us, it gives us access to the affective attachments that issue from its own aesthetic capability. That is the grandeur of cinema.

Much more could be said about the dialectic between failure and renewal in attachment as related to alienation. If we view all human existence as potentially a work of art, we can readily imagine how to extend these few remarks. But here I wish to move on to the two other concepts I mentioned.

Estrangement is a somewhat unpleasant, and often pathological, state in which we experience the world as foreign to whatever we consider "natural" or amenable to our existence. This condition is frequently induced by drugs or distilled alcohol, which are fairly modern devices. Centuries before their bizarre effect was first discovered, primitive people cultivated episodes of estrangement by ingesting special herbs or mushrooms, by dancing wildly to the point of stupor, and by engaging in extremely prolonged sexual behavior.

The conviction that we are strangers in our own reality and that it is basically strange to us bespeaks an affective failure on our part. It reveals an inability to feel at home in our surroundings. But it is also an accurate and authentic representation of a sense of division between body and mind, matter and spirit, that human beings often (always?) experience. As long as that feeling persists, above all when it is unrecognized because submerged in evasive tactics, we cannot have attachments that unite or harmonize body and mind, matter and spirit. Unless these attachments occur, the world is sure to seem strange to some degree.

The alcoholic, the drug addict, the whirling dervish, or the sex maniac do what they do in an attempt to ward off the sense of estrangement by paradoxically evoking it, as if they were vaccinating themselves. But we do not have to resort to such dangerous measures. The listening to ghost stories or the watching of horror films can have a similar effect for people who cultivate an interest in these art forms. The ability to engross oneself in such compensatory artifacts, and to savor a sufficient enjoyment of them, helps alleviate our fear that we are homeless in a universe that includes so much that is foreign to us. Most of science fiction revolves about our feeling of estrangement from realities that other animate beings might possibly experience and even comprehend but that far exceed our current condition. Through the artistry of this fiction we transcend our lingering sense of homelessness, just as the primitive shamans did. We affectively attach ourselves to the baffling world around us by entering into its mysteries symbolically and through the efficacy of aesthetic engagement.

This may only be a minimal success, but it can work wonders in itself. For some people fervent prayer can be efficacious in that way. A person kneeling before getting into bed each night may just be uttering words into the void, an empty and impersonal cosmos. But the uncanny frightfulness of our being in a universe that has no meaning can be allayed by the fact that these are *our* words and they are meaningful to *us*. They might have nowhere to go, and certainly the act of praying will not be acceptable to everyone. But those who feel the need for this verbal effort, and who practice it with sincerity, may sometimes find that it can institute—at least for them—the desired feeling of oneness.

Detachment, as opposed to alienation and estrangement, implies a prior existence of some viable attachment to areas of life other than the ones from which we feel isolated. The most impressive images of detachment that have remained with me are those I noticed years ago in street-scene paintings of the Italian renaissance. On the edge of a crowd filled with lively men and women walking in the street, an elegant and handsome youth observes the spectacle with apparent indifference. He stands apart from the others and seems to have little interest in what he sees. But there is also something in his posture—a slight backward curve of the upper torso or the placement of his arms akimbo—that signifies a proud refusal to let others know what exactly has caught his attention, or how much he cares about it. His nonchalance, which Castiglione called *sprezzatura* and strongly commended as a noble manner in the ideal courtier, suggests that this person lays claim to a rightful place in another setting, where he truly does belong. His body language asserts that he is an aristocrat who does not deign to show himself as a member of this crowd. Or possibly he is an artist, like the painter of the picture, looking for visual qualities that vulgar laymen cannot appreciate. Perhaps he is only a sexual marauder taking note of those among the passersby who may be likely prey. We have no way of knowing.

I am especially intrigued by this renaissance image of detached sophistication because it expresses both failure and success in affective attachment. Proclaiming their legitimacy in that separate and exclusive domain from which they come, the young men are not utter losers in the search for consummatory bonding. Nor is their snobbishness uncharacteristic of our species. But what one gains in being detached can also cause an inability to share, or truly understand, the lives of those who are being studied with such coolness at a distance. The detached young men may defend their attitude by reminding themselves of whatever hidden attachment makes them different, but that assurance may only be a form of compensation for affective goods withheld from these persons though evidently attained by the people they are watching. The state of detachment incorporates both possibilities. It reverberates within their dialectic.

It is not fortuitous that I find my example of detachment in works of art. Whenever the aesthetic attitude occurs, it is itself a conscious detachment from the rest of life. It reconstitutes responses that usually belong to the purposive, and often humdrum, activities by which we manage to survive. As I have argued repeatedly, the aesthetic is foundational to all human values and to spirit as a whole. But its generic importance appears most obviously in what we demarcate as "art" or "the fine arts." They are contrivances for effecting the detachment that may reattach us to the reality of our humanhood. This alone justifies their systematic variance from the other values that matter to us.

We are so habituated to spending time looking at static objects in a museum or listening to artificial sounds in a concert hall that we forget how much we are thereby detaching ourselves from what is loosely called "the real world." Artists like Brecht in the theater or Miró in painting carefully instill this sense of separation in order to increase our awareness of the aesthetic truths their works convey.

Far from causing a failure to live in ordinary existence, they promote attachments to it engendered by the artful detachment they themselves create.

More than any previous philosopher, perhaps, Santayana understood both the natural and the spiritual implications of detachment. In one place he rightly says that "genuine detachment presupposes attachment."[2] But when he argues that spirit is always and necessarily detached from material nature, though stemming from it, Santayana confuses detachment with estrangement and alienation. He ignores spirit's ability to suffuse organic life with the goodness it itself comprises. Creative people recognize the importance of solitude and even inaccessibility because they know that these enable them to achieve the vital attachments that are often throttled in society.

Santayana's own detachment from other people empowered him to do work that negated the alienation and estrangement he experienced throughout his life. His genius consisted in knowing how to use the ricochet between detachment and attachment as an aesthetic resource in his writing, thus transforming his personal sense of isolation into superlative insights about the human predicament. His achievement in this endeavor belies his pessimistic claim that spirit can never escape its alienation and estrangement from the rest of life. He did not fully recognize that detachment such as his not only presupposes a prior and more fundamental attachment but also that it illustrates how affective failure of this sort can result in a heightened and correlative reattachment to the very world from which one felt so painfully separated.[3]

❋

As another avenue of speculation about affective failure and renewal, consider the fact that in the United States today, as

I am writing at the beginning of the twenty-first century, the attachments related to traditional monogamous marriage have diminished more than ever before. Concepts of interpersonal love passed on by the romanticism of the nineteenth century have been thoroughly undermined in the imagination of many young men and women. Since great exposure to sexual pleasures in early life can often dull our appetite for them, it is as if these people have aged prematurely with respect to love as well. Though the fear of sex and love has existed as long as human beings have desired and pursued them, that type of trepidation has become more extensive than earlier in modern civilization. Whether or not this trend is calamitous, it shows how new cultural values are defining our humanity through new patterns of mating and of bonding, new meanings of love and sexuality that life is now generating.

The failure of affective attachments must always be gauged in terms of the novel conditions and alternate rewards that progressively mold the being of our species. What is lost through separation and divorce may be balanced, conceivably, by greater freedoms that the former spouses can then acquire. Whether full or partial, these freedoms may constitute a state of greater opportunity, or else a well of desolation and agonizing loneliness. I leave it to psychologists and sociologists to document the likely consequences for individual or social well-being. What primarily interests me is the nature and significance of affective failure or success attainable by men and women under these conditions.

Imagine a hypothetical, but not unrepresentative, marriage that has lasted a long time. In their life together the spouses have shared many moments of struggle and achievement in relation to each other as well as to their social world. They have engaged in joint enterprises that may have flourished but were sometimes stressful and embittering. They have raised children who dealt with their own problems by draining the energies of their parents, if only in the process of trying to emancipate themselves from their authority. In the years of marriage the spouses have gone through personality changes that they could not always recognize. Eventually, and periodically in previous crises, they might have felt that their marital attachment was disintegrating. Since their responses to each other are now somewhat habitual and lacking in vivacity, they wonder why they should submit any longer to the constraints of matrimony.

I offer this brief vignette as a schematic portrait of what happens in many marriages. The question I ask is whether the affective attachments that might clearly have existed and been advantageous in former years can be described as having completed their proper course for these individuals. Given what human relationships are inherently, did theirs decline because its preordained life span had been accomplished, the warranty having run out, so to speak? Or should we say, more cynically, that it was only a matter of time before its irremediable though hidden fragility, present in almost all marriages, could rise to a level of painful awareness? The oneness this couple thought they were experiencing may never have been truly there. At the moment of break-up, husband and wife might feel that they should never have married in the first place, that they remained together not because they were well matched but only for adventitious reasons.

In some instances this diagnosis of marital failure is doubtless accurate. Are we sure, however, that we can know that it applies in any particular case? Despite the evidence of tension and emotional strain pervading a marriage—even from the very start, sometimes—we might cite the fact that these two people *did* stay together, for better and for worse, through family struggles that greatly mattered to them at the time and that they weathered in the company of each other. As years went by, their lives took on the tincture of their joint existence. Their actions and their feelings were imbued with the values of the marital partner in terms of whom they normally identified themselves. If their current suffering becomes too intense, they may plausibly conclude that the amatory bond has decayed beyond repair. Yet they are what they are because of their mutual history. They cannot discard it as they would a fruit that has fallen to the ground and become overly ripe. They cannot ignore its permanent effect upon themselves or, in most cases, upon the children they produced.

There is something Orson Welles said at the end of his film career that is worth pondering at this point. Lamenting that his life as a moviemaker consisted in 98 percent hustling for money and only 2 percent in actually making films, Welles remarked: "I think I made essentially a mistake in staying in movies. But it's a mistake I can't regret because . . . it's like saying: 'I shouldn't have stayed married to that woman, but I did because I loved her. I would have been more successful if I hadn't been married to her.'"[4]

Welles means that as a careerist he would have had a more successful life if he had not directed movies but rather limited himself to being an actor or writer or even politician. Despite his failures and frustrations as a filmmaker, he nevertheless recognizes his affective attachment to the making of films. That he does not regret. His marriage analogy would seem to trade upon the fact that spouses sometimes give supreme importance to the love they experience in matrimony even if it entails major losses in other areas. But what if the failure, frustration, and relative unhappiness come from the love itself, over and above the sacrifices caused by their life as a couple? Can married people claim that a love that is present despite the miseries in their relationship outweighs their regrets about the marital origin of these sorrows?

An affirmative answer to such questions is paradoxical. It implies that even a bad marriage, one that ought to be dissolved, would have to be welcomed, at least retained, if only it has been held together by love. Does love justify all consequences of it? Should we not condemn any love that perpetuates suffering that divorce and a new beginning with someone else can totally abolish? On the other hand, the unhappy spouses might well conclude that the love that has made them what they are, for worse if not for better, may be itself a consummation that one should cherish in a world that is not overflowing with opportunities for love that does succeed.

That conclusion is embodied in the joke about the man who tells a friend that after many years of marriage he and his wife have reached a point where they feel hatred toward each other. The friend is scandalized. "That's terrible," he says. "You must get a divorce and marry another woman." "What!" the first man exclaims, "And hate a stranger!" Shakespeare addresses a similar problem in the sonnet that declares that love does not alter when it alteration finds, but rather "bears it out even to the edge of doom."[5] As in the joke, this recognizes that love is not a garden of pure delights. It is a condition that may be fraught with failure and emotional defeat emanating from within itself. The married life to which it contributes can be far from ideal. And yet its continuance is sometimes preferable to solutions that eradicate suffering but also remain unproved as possibilities in which authentic love may or may not occur.

If we hate another person, we have emotional access to him or her. That gives love a chance to develop. Unless it is too intense, the failure present in hatred may be a blessing in disguise.

For this reason, it seems odd to say that the couple I mentioned were either deluding themselves throughout their marriage or else discovering now that its life span has been exceeded. Human nature is more intricate and confusing than these alternatives would suggest. They are much too simplistic to serve as persuasive explanations of an affective failure. However felicitous love may be, it cannot escape the difficulties that recur throughout all intimate relations. When these difficulties are too burdensome, given each person's individual capacity, the bonds of matrimony will be noticeably impaired. As affective attachments, however, they may endure if the spouses realize and appreciate the extent to which their existence together has made them what they are. That is something they have mutually created.

In adherence to this factuality, the couple may choose a renewal of their endangered attachment. But this commitment is a bestowal they need not make. They are always free to renounce their marriage, as they are also free to repudiate the past. There is no assurance that they can ever attain absolute clarity about what they *really* want. It involves an understanding of their affective failure, and sometimes— though not necessarily—a refusal to feel any special piety toward their present state of being. Whatever they decide, the situation is likely to be agonizing.

Fidelity to marital attachments is a virtue that has been enshrined in the pantheon of most civilizations. If it is not the only option countenanced by their society, however, the spouses may often feel justified in ranking personal freedom higher than fidelity. But neither freedom nor fidelity can be given a prior supremacy in all cases. In any event, we generally choose between them on the basis of inclination rather than reason. Only rarely, if ever, can both be satisfied simultaneously. That is part of the imperfection and unavoidable incompleteness that results from being human.

We tend to ignore this harsh truth because our feelings are so easily given to hopes of a culminating interpersonal oneness. Affective failure preceding, and leading into, emotional success is a pattern that fiction has often glamorized. Having met under trying circumstances, the 'young man and woman feel at first nothing but reciprocal repugnance or indifference. Like members of other species, they may have knowledge of advantages to be found in the opposite gender, but as yet that does not bond them as a natural pair. They are distrustful of anyone who intrudes upon their personal territory, much as a female herring gull will attack a male who wanders into her plot of land. To assure her that his intentions are matrimonial, the male herring gull appeases the female through nonaggressive and largely ceremonial gestures. But human beings often defeat this model. They are too proud, too quick to take offense, too greatly driven by schemes of the intellect, or by idealizations derivative from these schemes. If they manage to overcome their initial disaffection, the couple may do so only after they are thrown together in joint combat with people or material nature inimical to them both.

Having been united against their will by brute necessity, having lived at close quarters throughout the hardships imposed by unavoidable happenstance, having survived and even won out despite extreme obstacles, the man and woman finally decide that they were meant for each other. In the many literary or cinematic variations upon this motif, a favorite among novels and movies in every age and in every country, the two young people now declare they love each other. They passionately embrace, and that completes their story. We learn nothing more about them. The rest is silence, which is to say that the adventure of establishing their bond has found its consummation. They have proved themselves worthy as human beings by fulfilling the idealized parameters of their romantic attachment.

This analysis of affective failure and renewal in marriage may amplify what I said about cosmic love. Much of our life in nature is not the same as going through the joys and anxieties of marriage, but the basic structures are not dissimilar. Both begin with a period of innocent aspiration. In whatever surroundings provided by our society and the world in which we live, both progress through explorations that are chastening, though sometimes very gratifying. We soon learn how obdurate facticity can be. The great tradition of nineteenth-century realist fiction, as in Balzac, Stendhal, Turgenev, and Henry James, devotes itself to a succession of imaginative variations on this theme.

Since the world is never ideal, but only a nexus of brute occurrences arising from determinants that are generally random and often uncontrollable, no attachment can be objectively ordained or perfectly benign. The best of marriages may retain vestiges of their original romantic ardor, and these can blossom into parental consummations that are worth any incidental sacrifice or loss of freedom. In payment for these consummations, we may be willing to incur whatever seems required. But since the price can be quite substantial, that itself may be taken as a form of failure. In any event, the frequency of optimal attachments is never very great, though of course the statistics will vary for different persons and at different moments in history.

Our entire immersion in nature is subject to vicissitudes of a kindred sort. And yet the analogy is misleading in one important detail. While there are undoubtedly marriages that start out well and then flourish until one or the other partner dies, we can never expect to have that kind of relationship with nature. It is not just a matter of our being finite creatures. A good marriage is also finite, and possibly predicated upon a recognition of its finitude. But marital affection, like interpersonal love as a whole, is just an element in life. It cannot be all of one's existence. Even when it beautifully succeeds, a happy marriage does not eliminate our need to struggle with the environment and to face our coming death. The consummations that issue from affective attachments to a spouse, a family, a society, or to humanity at large cannot displace the hazards that result from the mortality of our existence.

Though we speak of "Mother Nature," we know that she is mainly foreign to us, a potential enemy as well as a kindly purveyor of goods, a destroyer of our being as well as a source and sustenance of it before our destruction. More than any actual mother, nature is ambivalent in the love she extends to us. To be ourselves, we must separate from our biological mothers at an appropriate time in our development. But there is no separation from nature. We always depend on its shifting and limited support, despite our everpresent sense of being partly alienated from it.

❊

Orthodox religion has customarily sought to alleviate the pressure of this misfortune by presenting to our imagination the possibility of a Being who is greater than nature, who outranks it ontologically and who offers total, even eternal love beyond its capability. Having on our side such a friendly presence, conceived to be the correction as well as the progenitor of nature's ambivalence toward us, we are encouraged to hope for endless consummation through a transcendental attachment that death itself cannot terminate.

In rejecting this conception, atheists like Schopenhauer and Nietzsche formulate paths of salvation that parallel those envisaged by traditional religions. Schopenhauer thinks that only nay-saying, which is in effect the same as Lucifer's defiant "Non serviam," can liberate us from abject submission to nature. Though our residual dependence upon it remains disastrous, a calamity that is inescapable he believes, Schopenhauer recommends spiritual detachment as the only way to achieve a sense of dignity. In advocating yea-saying, Nietzsche would seem to be more healthy-minded than Schopenhauer. He is certainly more optimistic, despite his equal lack of theological faith.

Yet Nietzsche's stance may be deceptive. Reviling the Schopenhauerian outlook, Nietzsche says in one place that Schopenhauer was not himself a real pessimist. How can that be? Because, Nietzsche tells us, Schopenhauer would eat a hearty breakfast, cheerfully spend his mornings on his writing, after lunch go for a walk with his dog, and then have a good dinner in the evening and play on the flute with great delight. That's not what it is to be a pessimist, Nietzsche concludes. But I think Schopenhauer would reply that Nietzsche has missed the point. If we accept the truthfulness of pessimistic philosophy, Schopenhauer would say, we do not suffer from false expectations, we do not yearn for attachments or consummations that the universe will not provide, we do not strive for inflated or fallacious ideals that no one can attain. Sooner or later, the deluded idealist will be engulfed in a sense of failure, and even convinced of his own worthlessness.

The true pessimist avoids such degradation and freely enjoys whatever goodness he or she can garner from taking the pleasures of our existence as they come. One thereby outwits nature while rising above its inherent vileness. That is the meaning of what Schopenhauer defines as being spiritually detached. He himself had a reasonably contented existence, and he lived to a ripe old age for the nineteenth century. Nietzsche, who became increasingly embittered by his outcast state, was sickly and unhappy throughout most of the forty-seven years before his final breakdown.

The question about our ability to love reality in itself preoccupied Hegel as well as Schopenhauer and Nietzsche. Hegel thought that everything that exists is marching, in the broken and sometimes halting manner of the empirical world, toward Absolute Spirit. He modeled this view upon the Christian notion that in creating everything God is always drawing it all toward his own perfection. Nevertheless, Hegel rejected the orthodox belief that God (the Absolute) precedes existence in the order of temporality. That God's love is in the world though his being is essentially outside it had been a puzzlement that Western, as well as Eastern, religion had grappled with for centuries. Hegel's solution consisted in the idea that the Absolute has no prior being but creatively evolves through the dynamic, and dialectic, realities that occur in time and seek to transcend themselves by their constant striving for the perfect ideality which is the Absolute.

Schopenhauer and Nietzsche spurned Hegelian idealism because they wanted to insist upon the fact that most, and possibly all, of nature is repugnant to ideals that human beings nurture. They thought our imagination and idealization—to say nothing of our intellect—lead us to distrust the cosmos. Far from being affectively attached to it, we must feel horrified by its hostility toward the goals we mainly care about. Even Nietzsche, who reverts to Hegel's buoyant activism as an antidote to Schopenhauerian detachment, would never say that amor fati, our ability to love hideous nature indiscriminately, is a manifestation of God or the Absolute coming into existence as an emergent perfection. On the contrary, Nietzsche agreed with Schopenhauer, as I do too, that love of any type is an ideal manufactured by ourselves, as mere mortals in nature. But this alone cannot support a belief in amor fati. Is there anything else that can?

One might try to rectify the defects in the Nietzschean concept by seeing it as a standard that is ethical rather than cosmic in scope. At various times Nietzsche portrays amor fati as an admirable reaction to events that adversely affect one's life. To be godlike and to love ourself properly, he says, we must treat these occurrences as opportunities for moral response on our part. Bad as any of them may be, "it remains within our power to use each event . . . for our improvement and fitness, and as it were to exhaust it."[6] To this extent, amor fati consists in our ability to welcome and affirm everything that has happened to us, everything we have become. We accept our world as a reality that we can now accommodate by changing it for the better. We love all things, evil though many of them are, insofar as we accept them as having made it possible for us to act like heroes by doing whatever we can in courageously dealing with our lot.

This reading of Nietzsche on amor fati emphasizes a characteristic strand that fills much of his writings. He often sounds as if all events in personal life are worthy of being loved if only we can use them to bolster our search for self-perfection. That strengthens us as creators of our destiny. If this were the entire burden of Nietzsche's conception, however, one could reply that what he depicts is not love of fate, and may not even be love. It is not an acceptance of events as they happen to exist, but only an appraisive estimation of how we may benefit from them. Though this might improve us morally, it can scarcely constitute a love of the events as they are in themselves. There would be no bestowal of value upon their individual being, no love of them apart from their serendipitous advantage to us. Our attitude would just be egocentric.

In most of his pronouncements about amor fati, Nietzsche seems to be seeking a nonegocentric kind of love. But he usually presents it as a love of self. In *The Gay Science*, for instance, he states: "I want to learn more and more to see as beautiful what is necessary in things; then I shall be one of those who make things beautiful."[7] This ambiguity, or confusion, in Nietzsche's thinking recurs throughout his philosophy.

To get a further leverage on this issue, Spinoza's ideas are worth examining. Over and above the rationalist tradition that he accepts, Spinoza was a precursor for Nietzsche as well as Schopenhauer and Hegel, and indeed for much of the nineteenth-century romanticism with which they all intersect. Spinoza's references to the "intellectual love of God" were designed to show how we can have an affirmative attachment to the entire universe. His saying that God is nature appears in conjunction with his distinction between "*natura naturata*" and "*natura naturans*." While the former includes events, processes, things, and people as they exist in the temporality of the empirical world, the latter is all of nature taken as an organic whole. Spinoza insisted that God is not natura naturata; he is not in the world as we are in it, or as any other particularities are. God is present in nature, and is identical with nature, Spinoza thought, only insofar as nature is envisaged under the aspect of its totality.

God or Nature, to use the locution that caused Spinoza to be excommunicated by his synagogue in Amsterdam, he characterized as the uniform and all-inclusive reality of everything that does or can occur. Through science and enlightened philosophy we may comprehend both the oneness and the diversity within this universal structure. We become affectively attached to it through the correct employment of reason. Through dedication to the truth about nature, human beings experience a love of God that is purely intellectual and wholly exempt from any personal selfishness. According to Spinoza, this is the highest form of love and possibly the only one that is defensible. Spinoza does not portray the dimensions of this grand attachment in any detail, but I think one can fairly say that he believed all justifiable types of love must be derivative from it.

Earlier in this book, I criticized the essentialism that reduces love to a mode of cognition, or limits it to any of its varieties, or assigns it to a search for universal truths. Despite the fervent naturalism that enriches Spinoza's philosophy, it seems to me tarnished by the essentialistic rationalism that he affirmed, like most other thinkers in the seventeenth century, and tried to express *in modo geometrico*. His synthesis was bold and imaginative, but we must go beyond it.

❆

Spinoza's influence on the romanticism of later centuries is a topic for scholarly study whose fruitfulness has not been exhausted. Espousing a love of nature, at least natura naturans, combined with unremitting trust in scientific reasoning, Spinoza paved the way for the adulation of science and technology to which our own era has so greatly adhered. His ideas provided a quasi-religious foundation for the world outlook of many professionals in the last two hundred years. The prevailing attitude of these people is tinged with romanticism inasmuch as that extolled absolute and even impassioned devotion to inquiries that probe the secrets of the universe.

Unlike Schopenhauer or even Nietzsche, whose romanticism was anti-Romantic, Spinoza does not consider nature a threat to human values. He does not recoil from it as a meaningless process that creates and then destroys life. Goya's painting of Saturn devouring one of his sons would have made no sense to Spinoza. Indeed he commends science not as a path of salvation that detaches us from nature, and thus transcends it to that extent, but rather as a loving revelation that displays how magnificently the laws of nature cooperate among themselves.

Spinoza could have this rosy and approbative attitude because he felt assured that reason, untrammeled by medieval bigotry or ecclesiastic delusion, can and will progressively find the truth about reality. Intellectual love of God was itself the demonstration of this assurance. Spinoza's faith in the glorious power of cognition lives on as a vital impulse for contemporary scientists who may otherwise feel unconnected to the benign romanticism of the nineteenth century. Like Spinoza, many of them believe that science moves step by step toward complete knowledge about empirical factuality. Each generation of investigators is seen as making its piecemeal accretion in this linear progression. As long as science strictly and tirelessly remains faithful to the methods of valid reasoning, it brings us that much closer to the absolute comprehension that defines its mission.

Pursuing this ideal, scientists may feel that they are members of a vast army that unites the present with past and future efforts to understand all things in nature as they really are. This feeling is articulated as follows in a book for laymen that a well-known biologist has recently published: "Science offers the boldest metaphysics of the age. It is a thoroughly human construct, driven by the faith that if we dream, press to discover, explain, and dream again, thereby plunging repeatedly into new terrain, the world will somehow become clearer and we will grasp the true strangeness of the universe. And the strangeness will all prove to be connected and make sense."[8]

I myself have no such faith. I interpret this scientific creed as a religion of reason that is not entirely rational. It is an affective attachment to the cosmos as open in its entirety to human intellect, and capable of being analyzed by it. The goal of such attachment, for which some investigators may even offer themselves as martyrs, is the eventual discovery of rock-bottom, certain, and irrefutable knowledge about the whole of natural being. Though the enterprise may take many centuries, eons perhaps, those who dedicate themselves to it at any stage feel they can take pride in having contributed to their cause. I have never felt a need to emulate them.

Observing the spectacle of this cognitivist devotion, I feel awe in the face of such unswerving confidence. The saintliness of Spinoza, both as a person and as a philosopher, seems undeniable to me. The clean and fervent attitude of aspiring scientists, many of whom I have watched in the making during my years at MIT, fills me with more than superficial respect. But I have my reservations about the cosmic attachment that they intuitively seek, as Spinoza did explicitly throughout his life. I believe that their idealistic craving may evince an underlying affective failure. And if their quest for knowledge is faulty in that respect, the values it embodies will have to be reconstructed.

The picture of the universe proffered by Spinoza, and by those scientists who begin with premises similar to his, is not uncommon in the modern world. It is imaginatively presented in Ibsen's play *Peer Gynt*. The protagonist leaves his native land because he feels sure he can never find the truth about himself there. The Boyg, a strange voice he hears in a neighboring swamp, tells him to "go round" and so he wanders for years from country to country. His adventures bring him no closer to his reality than if he had remained at home. In a moment of despair he peels an onion in the hope of learning what it is at heart. To his chagrin he finds that this one has no heart. He finally concludes that the Boyg misled him and that the truth might have been more accessible if he had stayed where he was born. For Peer Gynt, however, time has now run out.

We can take Ibsen's parable as a negative commentary upon modern attempts to achieve oneness with the universe through scientific methodology. The scene with the onion is especially devastating. No matter how much science may peel away, its efforts will be futile if they are meant to give unitary and all-embracing knowledge about some underlying core of nature. Leaving aside the fact that this endeavor would have to be continued into some indefinitely remote future, what can substantiate the supposition that reality lends itself to any such belief about its inner constitution? Though mankind cannot bear too much uncertainty in its conception of ultimate being, how do we know that nature or reality as a whole will ever be comprehensible to us? If we assume without evidence that there *may* or *must* be an absolute completeness, an empirical possibility of attaining through scientific investigation some final knowledge about everything, our reasoning is merely circular.

On the other hand, as W. V. Quine once said to me in a related context, the circle is a much maligned figure. Circularity in some areas, and at some levels of speculation, may be useful as well as unavoidable. Though I think that is true, I want to inspect the circular beliefs that have served in the last few hundred years as part of the secular religion of many scientists. In thinking about themselves as soldiers in the great army that progressively amasses more pieces in the jigsaw puzzle they imagine nature to be, they posit that an integral picture is there to be found. Since it is now deeply obscured, covered over by layers of ignorance or obfuscation that science must eradicate, the metaphor built into the term *rock bottom* reveals their operative faith in what they are looking for. The metaphysical credence, and the a prioristic hope, of those who feel this faith is fueled by conviction that the universe does have a rock bottom that persistent inquiry can in principle disclose.

A religious, or quasi-religious, crusade of this sort has lured investigators on from discovery to discovery, from hypothesis to further hypothesis, from nascent observation to more abstract but still verifiable conceptualization. The beckoning ideal functions as all ideals do. It gives meaning to activities that might have been unfocused and disoriented without it. Moreover, it has succeeded in generating subsidiary ideals that become significant for theorists in different scientific fields: ideals that define the goals of physics or chemistry or whatever, and above them all, the ideal of a unified science. When the individual pursuits can be shown to interpenetrate in their discoveries as well as in their separate methodologies, it is thought, we will have made a giant step toward deciphering the cosmic code in at least its broadest outline. We will then be getting close to that rock-bottom information that has lured science onward.

As a humanist who lives in the company of scientists, I often encounter this faith as it shows itself between the lines of what its followers say, and as it illumines the beam in their peering eyes. Not only do I admire their sterling courage but also I recognize the affective import of this religion for men and women who are sustained by it. But I do not endorse its ingredient mythology. I see it as possibly a grand illusion, capable of precluding the very attachment to nature and our reality that science tries so diligently to bring about. I fear that the undue reliance upon reason may be creating a *vicious* circle, one that is counterproductive and even self-defeating.

❄

Articulating another, though equally circular, faith, I offer a vision that hews more closely to actual experience. The history of science and technology has consisted of stupendous growth in our knowledge about the world as well as our capacity to use such knowledge constructively. Nevertheless, this advance has not proceeded as former theorists anticipated. The more we have learned in the last four hundred years the more we have had to face new and previously unsuspected problems requiring collateral inquiry. Though science is very adept in expanding the range of its explorations, it still cannot answer, may be no nearer to answering, the fundamental questions about our existence. Progress in physics, biology, psychology, and the other scientific subjects has increased our knowledge without being able to assure us that we are on the way to learning everything that we want to know. It is not just a matter of finding that the more we discover the more we realize that much must still be discovered. Of greater significance is the fact that we have come to recognize as systematic our inability to determine *how much more* remains unknown and may possibly be unknowable by us.

As a corollary of their assumption that the universe is either fixed or developing within coordinates set in place by unchanging laws of nature, earlier scientists could reject as merely preanalytic all intimations of chance or haphazard occurrence. These were not allowed to dislodge the orderliness of the conceptual scheme. Since reason proceeds through discrete configurations of its own, one could well affirm that (in principle) it can explain any empirical realities. Given world enough and time, science would someday finish its task of unraveling the entangled mysteries in the cosmos.

But once we sense that the universe may not be as orderly as was thought, once we appreciate the apparent endlessness of questions to be asked, of questions that are themselves occasioned by interim answers we have accepted, once we realize how chaotic and randomly creative so many events in nature turn out to be, our expectation of ever reaching cognitive finality through scientific methods may well be shaken. At this point the more modest approach that I suggest can possibly recommend itself for consideration.

Everyone knows by acquaintance what the world of our own experience is like. It is, to some degree, what William James said about the mental content of an infant—a booming, buzzing confusion. Later maturation does not alter this condition entirely. It is merely transformed by the intelligence or ratiocination that intellect employs to help us make our way through the world around us. Perennial puzzles remain beyond our understanding. Regardless of how much we learn about the universe, we must treat them as a constant of our existence. That is why wonder is, for us, the beginning of wisdom.

We can go on speculating about these unresolved mysteries, and in fact our life would have no meaning unless we did. But aside from the material goods that technology creates as by-products of scientific achievement, the utility that derives from either our knowledge or our quest for better theories is largely aesthetic. We accrue, and we augment, the aesthetic value of science and technology by studying whatever problems lurk behind the ones we have already solved. As long as we continue to search imaginatively, we increase our enjoyment of the cognitive pursuits that we engage in from moment to moment. They become affective attachments in themselves, attachments that provide their own consummations—which are often quite substantial—apart from any metaphysical or ulterior motivation.

This approach to human experience differs from the one that Spinoza or more recent rationalists cultivate throughout their philosophy. What I am suggesting is not geared to a possible oneness with nature as a known or knowable totality. On the contrary, my view assumes the likely failure of any aspiration toward that kind of attachment. Since we are the products of a universe that has not been fully made, and that may never be in any conclusive manner, we can have the equivalent of cosmic love only in our minute though often gratifying ties to the world that directly impinges on us.

As I confessed, my position is just as circular as the one I am opposing. But mine demarcates a more limited circularity than the traditional views that have been dominant thus far and generally too presumptive. I would like to reawaken both scientific and religious minds to the immediacy and potential goodness of our experience, thoroughly baffling as it often is even when we give meaning to it. In art and the aesthetic dimension of all thinking about reality, this meaningfulness emerges from the power of imagination and idealization. They fashion and embellish whatever there is in nature that reveals itself to us. Though we cannot know, or attain any affective unity with, the cosmos as long as we seek a rock bottom of its being, we may garner other and, I think, preferable consummations when we accept nature as it appears in our varied interactions with it.

When that happens, the mere *doing* of science—however specialized it may be—turns into an artistic activity that is both precious and fulfilling. As in all of life that is good, the activity becomes valuable in itself and for its own sake. Human beings are very curious animals who like to tackle challenging problems. Science and technology are worth pursuing simply because they satisfy our curiosity while always providing new problems to be worked at. We need no other justification.

In the Bechtel Room at Harvard there is a portrait of William James that shows him clasping to his bosom a book or portfolio on the cover of which the following words appear: "Ever not quite." I take them as a philosophical utterance of his. They represent what I also feel about reality. At the end of his career, James called his conception of the world "radical empiricism" that tries to explain our place in the "pluralistic universe." If anyone wishes to use these terms to characterize my thinking about attachment and the affective vibrancy of our existence, I would not object.

Notes

Introduction: Affective Attachments

1. On recent work by psychologists on the nature of affect, see Eric Eich, John F. Kihlstrom, Gordon H. Bowers, Joseph P. Forgas, and Paula M. Niedenthal, *Cognition and Emotion* (Oxford: Oxford University Press, 2000); and Niko H. Frijda, "Emotions and Hedonic Experience," in *Well-Being: The Foundations of Hedonic Psychology*, ed. Daniel Kahneman, Ed Diener, and Norbert Schwarz (New York: Russell Sage, 1999), 190–210, particularly references on 193–96. See also Richard S. Lazarus, *Emotion and Adaptation* (New York: Oxford, 1991), 1–41, 194–203, and passim; and *Handbook of Emotions*, ed. Michael Lewis and Jeannette M. Haviland (New York: Guilford, 1993), particularly 223–431. On developments in psychiatric object–relations theory as the origin of attachment theory, see Jeremy Holmes, *John Bowlby and Attachment Theory* (London: Routledge, 1993), 1–10, 61–124, and passim.

2. The line in Yeats is: "How can we know the dancer from the dance?". ("Among School Children," stanza viii.)

3. See the following in *The Place of Attachment in Human Behavior*, ed. Colin Murray Parkes and Joan Stevenson-Hinde (New York: Basic Books, 1982); Mary D. Salter Ainsworth, "Attachment: Retrospect and Prospect," 2–30; Peter Marris, "Attachment and Society," 184–201; Robert S. Weiss, "Attachment in Adult Life,"

171–84. See also John Bowlby, *A Secure Base: Parent-Child Attachment and Healthy Human Development* (New York: Basic Books, 1988), 24–28 and 119–26.

4. Holmes, *John Bowlby and Attachment Theory*, 67.

5. On this, see Irving Singer, *The Pursuit of Love* (Baltimore: The Johns Hopkins University Press, 1994), 52–70.

6. On further ideas about pansexualism, see my book *Sex: A Philosophical Primer* (Lanham, Md.: Rowman & Littlefield, 2001), 33, 122–23.

7. On developments in my thinking about appraisal and bestowal, see the following writings of mine: *The Nature of Love: Plato to Luther* (Chicago: University of Chicago Press, 1984), 3–22; *The Nature of Love: The Modern World* (Chicago: University of Chicago Press, 1987), 390–406; *The Pursuit of Love*, passim; "A Reply to My Critics and Friendly Commentators," in *The Nature and Pursuit of Love: The Philosophy of Irving Singer*, ed. David Goicoechea (Amherst, N.Y.: Prometheus, 1995), 323–61.

8. Robin L. Harwood, Joan G. Miller, Nydia Lucca Irizarry, *Culture and Attachment: Perceptions of the Child in Context* (New York: Guilford, 1995), 7.

9. Friedrich Nietzsche, "The Dancing Song," in *Thus Spake Zarathustra*, trans. Walter Kaufmann (New York: Viking, 1966), 107.

Chapter 1: Imagination

1. See *The Nature of Love: The Modern World*, 401–6; and *The Nature and Pursuit of Love: The Philosophy of Irving Singer*, 326–28 and passim.

2. *American Masters* documentary, PBS, 1986.

3. See Martin S. Bergmann, *The Anatomy of Loving: The Story of Man's Quest to Know What Love Is* (New York: Columbia University Press, 1987), 159 and passim. In his "Three Essays on Sexuality," Freud says: "The finding of an object is in fact a refinding of it." *Standard Edition of the Complete Psychological Works of Sigmund Freud* (London: Hogarth Press and Institute of Psychoanalysis, 1964), 7:222. *Standard Edition* hereafter referred to as *SE*.

4. Ludwig Wittgenstein, *Philosophical Investigations*, ed. G. E. M. Anscombe (Oxford: Blackwell, 1953), 119–22, no. 391, also nos. 389–90 and 392–402.

5. Gilbert Ryle, *The Concept of Mind* (New York: Barnes and Noble, 1949), 257.

6. Jean-Paul Sartre, *The Psychology of the Imagination*, trans. Bernard Frechtman (New York: Citadel, 1965).

7. Edward S. Casey, *Imagining: A Phenomenological Study* (Bloomington: Indiana University Press, 1976), 116.

8. For further discussion and debate about philosophical as well as other types of theories about the nature of imagination, see Eva T. H. Brann, *The World of the Imagination: Sum and Substance* (Savage, Md.: Rowman & Littlefield, 1991). See also James Engell, *The Creative Imagination: Enlightenment to Romanticism* (Cambridge: Harvard University Press, 1981), and his entry on imagination in *The New Princeton Encyclopedia of Poetry and Poetics*, ed. Alex Preminger, T. V. F. Brogan, et al. (Princeton: Princeton University Press, 1993), 566–74; Mary Warnock, *Imagination and Time* (Oxford: Blackwell, 1994); and Sarah L. Gibbons, *Kant's Theory of Imagination: Bridging Gaps in Judgement and Experience* (Oxford: Clarendon, 1994).

Chapter 2: Idealization

1. On the relation between imagination and idealization, see also my book *The Harmony of Nature and Spirit*, vol. 3 of *Meaning in Life* (Baltimore: The Johns Hopkins University Press, 1996), 96–110 and passim.

2. See *The Harmony of Nature and Spirit*, 185–94. See also my chapter on Schopenhauer in *The Nature of Love: Courtly and Romantic*, particularly 461ff.

3. For a discussion of Proust on love, see my chapter on him in *The Nature of Love: The Modern World*, 159–218.

4. "The Kiss," *The Portable Chekhov*, ed. Avrahm Yarmolinsky (New York: Viking, 1947), 164.

5. *Portable Chekhov*, 176–77.

6. *Portable Chekhov*, 177.

7. *Portable Chekhov*, 179.

8. For a more comprehensive discussion of Freud on love in relation to idealization, see *The Nature of Love: Plato to Luther*, 23–38; also my chapter on Freud in *The Nature of Love: The Modern World*, 97–158; and comments about his views in *The Pursuit of Love*, passim.

9. See my chapter on Shelley in *The Nature of Love: Courtly and Romantic*, particularly 411–27. My quote is from "A Defence of Poetry."

Chapter 3: Consummation

1. Thomas Nagel, "Death," in his *Mortal Questions* (Cambridge: Cambridge University Press, 1979), 10.

2. See Mary Mothersill, "Death," in *Life and Meaning: A Reader*, ed. Oswald Hanfling (Oxford: Basil Blackwell, 1987), 83–92.

3. On this see Gregory Vlastos, *Socrates, Ironist and Moral Philosopher* (Ithaca, N.Y.: Cornell University Press, 1991), 21–44. See also Luis E. Navia, *Socrates: The Man and his Philosophy* (Lanham, Md.: University Press of America, 1985).

4. Jeremy Bentham, *Deontology, or the Science of Morals* (London: 1834), I:39, quoted in Navia, *Socrates*, 300.

5. Friedrich Nietzsche, *The Birth of Tragedy* in *The Birth of Tragedy and The Genealogy of Morals*, trans. Francis Golffing (New York: Anchor Books, 1956), 3–4.

6. See Ronald Hayman, *Thomas Mann: A Biography* (New York: Scribner, 1995); and Anthony Heilbut, *Thomas Mann: Eros and Literature* (New York: Knopf, 1996).

7. Among others who hold this view, see, Heilbut, *Thomas Mann: Eros and Literature*, passim; T. J. Reed, *Death in Venice: Making and Unmaking a Master* (New York: Twayne, 1994), passim; and Robert Tobin, "The Life and Work of Thomas Mann: A Gay Perspective," in *Thomas Mann: Death in Venice*, ed. Naomi Ritter (Boston: Bedford, 1998), 225–44.

8. Quoted in Heilbut, *Thomas Mann: Eros and Literature*, 452.

9. Thomas Mann, letter to Carl Maria von Weber, July 4, 1920, quoted in Hayman, *Thomas Mann: A Biography*, 250.

10. Quoted in Frank Harris, *Oscar Wilde* (New York: Dell, 1960), 175–76.

11. Thomas Mann, *Death in Venice and Seven Other Stories*, trans. H. T. Lowe-Porter (New York: Vintage, 1954), 50.

12. For further discussion of both Mann's novella and Luchino Visconti's film adaptation of it, see my book *Reality Transformed: Film as Meaning and Technique* (Cambridge, Mass.: MIT Press, 1998), 103–27.

13. See *The Pursuit of Love*, 51–70.

14. Quoted in Heilbut, *Thomas Mann: Eros and Literature*, 502.

15. Thomas Mann, *Diaries, 1918–1939*, trans. Richard and Clara Winston (New York: H. N. Abrams, 1982), 210.

16. For further discussion of the definition of homosexuality and bisexuality, see Eve Kosofsky Sedgwick, *Epistemology of the Closet* (Berkeley: University of California Press, 1990), 1–63; and David M. Halperin, "How to Do The History of Male Homosexuality," *GLQ: A Journal of Gay and Lesbian Studies*, 6.1 (2000): 87–123.

Chapter 4: The Aesthetic

1. Immanuel Kant, *Groundwork of the Metaphysics of Morals*, trans. H. J. Paton (New York: Harper & Row, 1964), 67.

2. See John Rawls, *A Theory of Justice*, rev. ed. (Cambridge: Harvard University Press, 1999).

3. See Robert C. Solomon, *A Passion for Justice: Emotions and the Origins of the Social Contract* (Reading, Mass.: Addison-Wesley, 1990), 198–241 and passim.

4. *The Family Mark Twain* (New York: Harper, 1935), 1190.

5. *Family Mark Twain*, 1188.

6. *Family Mark Train*, 1204.

7. Foreword by the Dalai Lama, in Mark Epstein, *Thoughts Without a Thinker: Psychotherapy from a Buddhist Perspective* (New York: Basic Books, l995), ix.

8. Sigmund Freud, *New Introductory Lectures on Psycho-Analysis*, in *SE*, 22:95. See also the discussion of this in Epstein, *Thoughts Without a Thinker*, 213–14.

9. Sigmund Freud, "Analysis Terminable and Interminable," in *SE*, 23:235.

10. Friedrich Nietzsche, *Ecce Homo*, in *On the Genealogy of Morals and Ecce Homo*, trans. Walter Kaufmann and R. J. Hollingdale (New York: Vintage, 1967), 258. See also my discussion in *The Nature of Love: The Modern World*, 79–83 and in *The Creation of Value*, vol. 1 of *Meaning in Life*, pp. xii–xiv, 21–23, 144–45.

11. Friedrich Nietzsche, *The Twilight of the Gods*, in *A Nietzsche Reader*, trans. R. J. Hollingdale (Harmondsworth, England: Penguin, 1977), 164.

Chapter 5: Affective Failure and Renewal

1. See *Reality Transformed*, 131–52 and passim.

2. George Santayana, *Persons and Places: Fragments of Autobiography*, ed. William G. Holzberger and Herman J. Saatkamp, Jr. (Cambridge, Mass.: MIT Press, 1986), 421.

3. For a more complete presentation of this way of interpreting Santayana's philosophy, see my book *George Santayana, Literary Philosopher* (New Haven, Conn.: Yale University Press, 2000).

4. BBC Television, *Orson Welles: Stories from A Life in Film*, 1989.

5. Sonnet 116.

6. Friedrich Nietzsche, letter dated February 2, 1867, trans. Leslie Paul Thiele and quoted in his book *Friedrich Nietzsche and the Politics of the Soul: A Study of Heroic Individualism* (Princeton: Princeton University Press, 1990), 198. On Nietzsche's concept of amor fati, see Thiele's book, 197–206.

7. Friedrich Nietzsche, *The Gay Science*, trans. Walter Kaufmann (New York: Vintage, 1974), 223.

8. Edward O. Wilson, *Consilience: The Unity of Knowledge* (New York: Vintage, 1999), 12. In relation to this faith in ultimate connectedness, see also the following recent books about the search for a "theory of everything" in current theoretical particle physics and theoretical cosmology: Brian Greene, *The Elegant*

Universe: Superstrings, Hidden Dimensions, and the Quest for the Ultimate Theory (New York: Vintage, 2000); and David Lindley, *The End of Physics: The Myth of a Unified Theory* (New York: Basic, 1993). The first of these renews the faith in an ultimate theory; the second argues that it constitutes a myth whose truth cannot be demonstrated: "The theory of everything, this myth, will indeed spell the end of physics . . . not because physics has at last been able to explain everything in the universe, but because physics has reached the end of all the things it has the power to explain" (255).

Index

217

About the Author

Irving Singer is the author of many books, including *Sex: A Philosophical Primer*; *George Santayana, Literary Philosopher*; *Reality Transformed: Film as Meaning and Technique*; and his trilogies, *Meaning in Life* and *The Nature of Love*. He is a professor of philosophy at the Massachusetts Institute of Technology.